12-20-74

Employment
Conditions
in
Europe

Margaret Stewart

Gower Economic Publications / Employment Conditions Abroad Ltd

First published in Britain by Gower Press Limited, Epping, Essex.

1972

© Employment Conditions Abroad Ltd

ISBN 0 7161 0166 1

GOWER ECONOMIC PUBLICATIONS

Gower Economic Publications is the subsidiary imprint of Gower Press specialising in the research and publication of economic reviews and locational studies. Each Review is regularly updated allowing for the inclusion of the latest statistical data and comments.

Managing Editor
A R Buckley BA

Typeset by The Pentagon Bureau, London
Printed in Great Britain by
Redwood Press Limited, Trowbridge, Wiltshire

Contents

1834862

List of Illustrations

Publisher's Preface

The countries surveyed for this publication correspond to the six existing members and the four proposed applicants to the Community as at summer 1972. The subdivisions within the book reflect this selection criteria with Part Two covering the surveys of the original members — Belgium, France, Germany, Italy, Luxembourg and the Netherlands — and Part Three dealing with the applicants — namely Denmark, Irish Republic, Norway and the United Kingdom.

All research efforts had been completed prior to the result of the Norwegian referendum of 26th September 1972 rejecting by a small majority the concept of Common Market membership. Given the completion of these research efforts it has been decided to retain material on this country within the publication. Its existence does in no way, however, reflect the possibility or otherwise of eventual Norwegian entry into the European Community.

EMPLOYMENT CONDITIONS ABROAD LIMITED

This survey was commissioned by Employment Conditions Abroad Ltd., an organisation established by a number of major international companies who are represented in some 140 countries. Its object is to collect, analyse and distribute up-to-date comprehensive and factual information about terms and conditions of employment throughout the world covering both expatriate and local employees.

The information covers such aspects as remuneration comparisons, allowances and fringe benefits, personal income tax, living costs and conditions and education resources for children. Many other aspects, such as employment legislation, labour availability, work permits and procedures, tax treatment of expatriate remuneration are also covered as well as the related background of the general political, financial, economic and industrial relations situation in each country.

The organisation is in the process of building up this data bank of information based on the network of communications provided from its own member companies, and collected from many other authoritative sources. A cost-of-living survey is being carried out in some ninety countries and will form the base of an independent index for the use of members.

The information services are designed specifically for the use of companies who have interests in countries outside their own home base, and is on a membership basis.

Full details can be obtained from:

J. H. G. Firth
Executive Director
Employment Conditions Abroad Limited
9 Orme Court
London W2 4RL
Telephone: 01-229 3262

Introduction

So many books, pamphlets, reports and articles have appeared and are appearing about the Common Market, and so much good advice is given to British businessmen about what to do and what not to do after January 1st 1973, that it may seem supererogatory to seek to add to the Niagara of information. But the purpose of this book is to centralise and co-ordinate much of the material that has appeared elsewhere, and to provide a series of factual signposts for executives of companies who are establishing themselves in the enlarged Community. It is almost entirely concerned with employment aspects, such as manpower, wages and working conditions, social security and labour relations, and is intended primarily to be of help to personnel managers and others who are concerned with labour relations. It may also help executives to decide which country to choose for their investment, by describing the different systems of financial incentive, the availability of labour and wage costs.

I have not touched on the political or institutional aspects of the European Economic Community, nor on commercial, monetary and agricultural policies.

The book is in two parts. Part I gives a brief account of the Commission's responsibilities in regard to labour and social policies and contains comparative tables.

Part II gives a country-by-country survey of employment conditions in the Six. Part III gives similar surveys for the four countries scheduled for EEC membership in January 1973. The length of each chapter varies according to the economic importance of the country but each follows the same broad pattern. This is to provide a general introductory background, followed by sections on manpower resources (with particular emphasis on regional differences), wages and social security, labour relations and procedures and collective bargaining.

The material has been collected from official and unofficial sources, interviews and personal visits to the EEC headquarters in Brussels and to a number of EEC countries. Three major problems, as well as many minor ones, have been encountered. First, it is extremely difficult to obtain comparable up-to-date international statistics. I have tried, wherever possible, to use figures relating to 1970/1, but am conscious of the constant need for up-dating in the light of rapidly changing circumstances. This particularly applies to social security and benefits. Secondly, discrepancies are often found in different sets of figures relating to the same subject, and there seems to be a need for "harmonisation" of statistics. Mostly I have used EEC sources. Thirdly, the problem of what currency to quote emerged sharply during the summer of 1972. I have mainly used national currencies though in some cases rates are quoted in £ sterling equivalents.

Appendices I and II contain a list of sources of information and of addresses both in London and the other countries of the Ten. The Annex gives a brief outline of redundancy procedures in the Six and the UK.

Every effort has been made to verify the accuracy of the information, to bring the material up to date and to avoid any expression of personal opinions. I am deeply indebted to all who have supplied me with information and helped in the research, but the responsibility for everything in the book is my own.

Acknowledgments

The author is much indebted to very many individuals and organisations for their help and advice in the compilation of this book, and for permission to draw on their material and expert knowledge for much of the factual information contained therein.

Particular thanks are due to the following for permission to draw on material which has appeared in books, surveys and publications. (The names of these publications are listed in Appendix I and some addresses in Appendix II.

Messrs Roger Broad and R.J. Jarrett
The Confederation of British Industry
The Coventry and District Engineering Employers Association
The Daily Telegraph Ltd
The Economists Advisory Group
Mr Derek Ezra, Chairman, National Coal Board
Her Majesty's Stationery Office
Industrial Co-partnership Association
Industrial Press Ltd
Institute of Personnel Management
Management Centre Europe, Brussels
Management Counsellors International, Brussels
Noble Lowndes International Ltd
Mrs S. Patterson, Community Relations Commission

Acknowledgements

Among the many individuals and organisations who have helped, thanks are due to:

Mr John Firth, Executive Director, Employment Conditions Abroad Ltd and members of its staff.

Mr Philip Spademan, OBE, British Oxygen Company Ltd, a Director of Employment Conditions Abroad Ltd.

The Department of Trade and Industry.

The Overseas Department of the Department of Employment.

The Information Office, European Economic Community, London.

Officials in the Information, Industrial, Free Movement of Labour, Social Harmonisation and other departments of the European Commission in Brussels, and of the European Investment Bank.

Mr Harold F. Rossetti, CB, Director, and Mrs G.M.Sampson, Librarian, International Labour Office, London.

M Marc Carriche, Public Information Department, ILO Geneva and officials in the Labour Law and Labour Relations branch, ILO, Geneva.

The Labour Attaches of the French, German and Italian Embassies in London, the Information departments of the Embassies of Belgium, the Netherlands, Denmark and Luxembourg, the Press Attache of the Irish Embassy.

Representatives of the Confederation of British Industry.

The Labour Attache at the British Embassy, Bonn, Mr E.C.M. Cullingford, CMG, Mr J.M. Heath Counsellor (Commercial) British Embassy, Bonn, Mr J.S. Vigors, Labour Attache, British Embassy, Brussels, and Mr G.D. Cossar, Labour Attache, Stockholm.

Mr I. Ferguson, Urwick International, Dusseldorf.

Mr Norman Crossland, BBC correspondent, Bonn.

Officials of the Federal Republic Press and Information division and of the Federal Ministry of Labour, Bonn.

Herr Dr Lindner, German Employers Federation, and his staff, Koln.

Herr Dr Fritze, German Trade Unions, Dusseldorf.

M Raphael Lagasse, Overseas International Organisation of Employers, Geneva.

Dr B. Sohns, Ministry of Social Affairs, The Hague.

Representatives of the Netherlands Employers Federation and the Trade Union centre NVV.

Thanks are also due to many people who have read the manuscript, to Count Antonini for help with Italian translations and to Dr and Mrs Talma for help with the Dutch translations.

Part One

European Background

1

The Role of the Commission

No British company which is contemplating going into Europe need fear the existence of a vast bureaucracy in Brussels, with a network of rules and regulations governing their day-to-day industrial activities and labour relations.

The Preamble to the Treaty of Rome declares that the general aim is to raise living conditions and working standards, while Article 117 refers specifically to the need for improvements 'so as to permit the equalisation of those conditions in an upward direction.' The Commission is the executive which carries out decisions taken by the Council of Ministers, the supreme policy-making authority for the European Economic Community. Its own powers are limited in the industrial and social fields, and member nations jealously guard their independence and their traditional practices. It can only advise on and influence developments, except in a few respects, where there are direct powers laid down in the Treaty.

In the field of labour, the most important of these powers concerns the free movement of labour. This was originally laid down in the Treaty (articles 48-51) and extended by measures adopted by the Council of Ministers in July 1968. The Treaty required that any discrimination between Community nationals 'as regards employment, remuneration or other working conditions' should be abolished by the end of 1969. In fact, free movement came into force 18 months before the scheduled date.

It means that any worker who is a citizen of any EEC country can take a job in any of the other countries and enjoy the same rights and conditions as their nationals. The only exception is a worker employed in public administration. An EEC worker does not need a work permit, or a visa, and is allowed to move about within the Community to look for work. The only requirement is a residence permit which is issued for a period of five years and is automatically renewable. (Residence permits may be refused for reasons of 'public order', security or health.)

Once they arrive in a Common Market country, nationals from member states enjoy full equality of treatment in respect of wages, terms of employment, social security and taxation. They have the right to send for their families and dependents, and to rent or own a house. They are eligible for election to workers' representative bodies.

The British Government has accepted the principle of free movement of labour, though it has asked for a five year transitional period for Northern Ireland. As from January 1st 1973, British workers will be able to move freely within the enlarged Common Market, just as workers from the other Nine will be able to come to Britain. Few authorities, however, expect any very rapid development of cross movements between the UK and the Continent.

In general, differences in climate, customs and traditions, together with language and housing difficulties, are likely to prove formidable obstacles to such mobility. Another barrier is the absence so far of any provision for the mutual recognition of vocational, professional and academic qualifications. The Commission is working out proposals for the recognition of the main professions.

In practice, the movement of workers within the Six has not been on the scale that was originally anticipated. Except for Italy, the EEC countries have experienced a persistent shortage of labour and only the Italians have migrated to any extent. The shortage has had to be met in most countries by the immigration of non-EEC workers, mainly from the Mediterranean countries. They enter a Community country under bilateral arrangements and do not come under the free movement system.

The manpower position in each individual country is examined in Part II, but the following table will indicate the situation within the Six.

The Commission has set up machinery for protecting the interests of both migrant and local workers. There is a tripartite consultative committee on migrant workers and in 1970 a consultative standing committee on employment was established, with representation of employers, unions, the Commis-

Annual averages except Germany and Netherlands		All foreign workers	Of which EEC nationals (mainly Italians)	Foreign Workers as percentage of total labour
Belgium	1970	208,000*	117,000*	5.5
France	1970	1,200,000	280,000	5.8
Germany	1971	2,241,000	530,000*	8.3
Italy	1970	39,000	12,000	0.2
Luxembourg	1970	33,000	26,000	23.0
Netherlands	1971	125,000	49,000	2.7
Community	1971	3,487,000*	1,015,000*	5.1

* Approximate or Estimate
Source: EEC and Bureau europeen de coordination

TABLE 1.1   Foreign workers in the six member countries

sion and member states. Another committee deals with the social security aspects of migration. Guidance on job opportunities is given to migrants, on the basis of monthly reports of vacancies which are circulated within the Community. There is a safeguard clause that if an influx of workers threatens the living and working conditions in a particular area, a Government can discourage immigration, but it must first seek the approval of the Commission and other member governments.

Another provision of the Treaty of Rome (article 119) which is universally applicable (in theory but not in practice) is the adoption of equal pay, defined as 'equal remuneration for the same work as between male and female workers.' The original intention was to implement this article by 1961, but in fact little progress was made and a survey in 1966 showed that there was a wide gap in earnings. In June 1970, the Commission noted that although equal pay had not been fully achieved, some progress had been made towards this objective in all the countries (see Table 2.5, p.22).

Two other articles in the Treaty relate directly to employment conditions. Article 80 urges member states to encourage the exchange of young workers within the Community. The first programme was launched in 1954 and about 4,500 young workers, between 18 and 30, benefit each year. It is probable that British employers will welcome this scheme and may seek help from the Industrial Training Boards to enable them to implement it.

Article 118 vests the Commission with responsibility for promoting 'closer collaboration in the field of technical and vocational training'. In 1963, the

Council of Ministers laid down the general principles for training and re-training policies. But, according to Roger Broad and R.J. Jarrett (Community Europe today, 1972) the programme has been held up because of the failure of the six Governments to agree on procedure. The Commission, which estimates that the present generation of school-leavers must be prepared to accept two or more changes of skill or craft during their working life-time, is engaged in drawing up common lists of skills for various crafts and trades.

More success has been achieved with retraining schemes for redundant and unemployed workers. During the early 1950s, the European Coal and Steel Community launched a scheme for retraining coal and steel workers. This took the form of a tiding-over allowance equal to 80-100 per cent of the workers' previous average wage, plus differential allowances to make up, for up to two years, any difference between old and new wage levels. Training is free and resettlement grants are available for men who move to new jobs. The cost is shared equally between the Commission and the Government concerned. In all 440,535 workers were assisted in these schemes, between 1954 and December 1971.

A European Social Fund was established in 1958 to perform the same functions for workers in other industries. It provided member countries with half the costs involved in retraining workers who were unemployed or threatened with unemployment, including resettlement and a tiding over allowance of up to 90 per cent of their previous wage. By the end of 1971, a total of 1,436,000 workers had been assisted.

Plans to turn the Social Fund into a more dynamic and effective instrument and to enable it to play a more positive part in meeting the challenge of structural and technological change, have been agreed, after prolonged debate. Instead of acting more or less as a 'clearing house', financing half the cost of retraining programmes initiated by Government, the Fund will itself mount training schemes for workers, before their jobs disappear, and will provide on-the-spot aid in areas of high unemployment.

The reformed Fund became operative early in 1972. Both sides of Industry are associated with it, and programmes will be co-ordinated with those for agricultural, industrial and regional development.

Another instrument for promoting regional development is the European Investment Bank, set up under the Treaty to assist balanced and stable development within the EEC. It makes loans for approved projects in the under-developed regions, and for the modernisation and reconstruction of industry. The Bank has contributed substantially towards improving the infrastructure in the Mezzogiorno (Southern) region of Italy. It also invests in priority technological activities, eg nuclear power stations, and promotes the mutual co-operation of enterprises of different member countries.

Regional development has become the burning issue of the 1970s, and the emphasis is now being laid on taking work to the workers, rather than taking workers to the work. It was not envisaged in the Treaty of Rome that the Commission should itself play a very direct part in helping the development of the poorer areas or should launch a common regional policy. This was regarded as primarily a national responsibility. But, since 1969, there has been much discussion about the need for more positive Community action. Not all the Commission's proposals have been accepted by the member Governments but one step agreed on is to limit the amount of investment in the richer areas.

Regional development was one of the main themes at a conference in Venice called by the Commission in April 1972 and attended by over 300 European industrialists, trade unionists and EEC officials. Mr Derek Ezra, chairman of the National Coal Board, posed the question — to what extent should there be Community policies to encourage investment in the under-developed regions by both public and private sectors?

He pointed out that of the Community's total budget, 86 per cent would be devoted to agriculture in 1971. 'I believe that the time may now be approaching when we should be thinking in terms of directing financial support to a much greater extent towards the encouragement of industrial developments in areas where the proportion of the population employed on the land is very high and rather less towards the direct support of agriculture' he said. 'What is needed is the allocation of substantially increased resources, both on a Community and a national basis, to the solution of the regional problem through the stimulation of a faster rate of industrial development in the less developed regions. If this is not done quickly, the social and economic imbalances will become more marked and act as a major restriction on the growth and wellbeing of the Community as a whole.'

Because of the crucial importance of the regional problem, considerable space is devoted in this book to the position in different countries, together with appropriate maps.

Parallel with, and complementary to, the need for creating more employment in Europe's under-developed areas, is the question of the treatment of workers who lose their jobs through technological change or a decline in the demand for their products. The whole problem of redundancy payments is now under review by the Commission and certain proposals for improving and coordinating national practices have been put to the Council of Ministers. A note on these proposals and on existing practices is contained in an Annex (p.203).

Progress towards achieving common policies for industry, technology and transport has been slow, both because of the high priority given to agricultural policy and of the past reluctance of member nations to co-operate and pool their resources. In the early 1970s, however, there was a realisation within the EEC of the need to achieve a greater degree of unification and to re-think industrial policies in the light of the world economic situation.

In March 1970, the Commission submitted to the Council of Ministers a memorandum on industrial policy which laid down certain objectives. These included the completion of the common market for goods, access to public contracts, the co-ordination of purchasing policies and the creation of a single market for technologically advanced products. It urged the removal of obstacles to the formation of trans-national companies, the unification of legal, financial and taxation systems, and measures to promote change and assist adjustment. Mr Christopher Layton (Chief Executive Officer to the Commission's Member for Industry), writing in European Community (April 1972) said 'There is no doubt that the fruits of the enlargement of the Community can only be gathered if we can move on from the present customs union to a more radical pooling of the technological resources of Europe and of the efforts made by governments to support and develop industry.'

A common policy for transport is expressly laid down in the Rome Treaty (article 3) but here again national divisions have impeded progress.

Only 15 per cent of community trade is covered by the system of Community licences designed to facilitate road transport between the Six. Bilateral agreements usually limit routes to only two countries, and are thus wasteful of capacity. There are different regulations for the weight and wheelbase of trucks, and wide variations in pricing of transport services. M. Albert Coppé, member of the Commission, however claimed in January 1972 that, following meetings of the EEC Transport Ministers, there had been considerable improvements and that the outlook for the year was 'satisfactory'.

One section of the Rome Treaty (articles 52-58) provides for the right of establishment and the freedom for any firm, branch, agency and individual to set up in business or provide services in any of the member states. To this end, companies are treated in the same way as individuals, and can establish themselves, provided they are incorporated in accordance with national laws and have either their office or main place of business within the Community. The Commission has suggested proposals for harmonising many aspects of company law, and has drafted plans for a new 'European' company law to facilitate cross-frontier mergers. This plan, still under discussion, is likely to prove controversial, as it includes provision for workers' representation, on

8

the German 'Mitbestimmung' lines, with a right to veto certain management decisions and to have full access to information on company affairs.

Since the establishment of the Common Market, there has been an expansion in the volume of foreign, particularly American, investment in the EEC. Before 1958, the UK attracted 46 per cent of all US investment in Europe, but by 1969, the British share was only 30 per cent while US investment in the EEC had increased to 49 per cent. This increase has been attributed to the higher profitability and growth rates of EEC countries.

British investment in the EEC countries has been substantial in recent years. All the EEC countries have shared in the flow of investment, although the rate for Italy remained relatively low. In recent years, about 70 per cent of direct investment has been in manufacturing industry, including chemicals, brewing and a wide range of engineering activities, with a further 25 per cent in distribution and 5 per cent in financial and other services.

It is significant that the book value of UK investment in the EEC is about £800 million, while that of EEC investment in the UK is about £358 million. It is also significant that total UK investment abroad is second only to that of the United States. These two facts give an idea of the wide base from which the United Kingdom should be able to increase its exports, while at the same time the gap between inward and outward investment demonstrates the need for active promotion of new investment in the UK.

Professor J. H. Dunning, writing in 'Government and Business' (December 1971) argues that Britain's entry into the EEC may attract more American investment to the UK, one obvious advantage being the common language. He also considers that there may be an increase in investment in the type of growth industries which can more conveniently be served by on-the-spot manufacturing than by exports, and which will enable the company to take advantage of the larger and more integrated market.

It is evident that an important development in the investment field will be the growth of multi-national, trans-frontier companies, and in increased arrangements to pool resources for joint technologically-based products. Examples of the latter trend are the Anglo-French 'Concorde' aircraft, the Airbus project between France and Germany, and the Anglo-Dutch-German plan for producing enriched uranium.

Apart from the long-established Anglo-Dutch Unilever and Shell groups, recent trans-frontier mergers include those between Germany's Agfa and Belgium's Gevaert for manufacturing photographic films, between Dutch and German aircraft builders Vokker and Vereinigte Flugtechnische Werke.

In 1972, four medium-sized European manufacturers in the Netherlands, Germany, Sweden and France combined in a Dutch holding company to produce standard model lorries in the five to twelve ton range, to be assembled and sold separately in each country. In many cases, mergers are proposed in order to strengthen European competitiveness against the United States. This was the origin of the Dunlop/Pirelli merger in 1970.

The trend towards multi-national organisations has given rise to trade union fears that companies will be able to switch production from one country to another, without regard for the social problems involved or the workers' interests. There have been moves to engage in multi-national bargaining and to present a common labour negotiating front. The pace-setters have been the International Federations of Metalworkers (covering engineering and vehicle industries) and Chemical workers (chemicals, atomic energy, cement, glass, ceramics, paper and rubber). In June 1972, negotiators from Ford plants in six European countries met to seek to establish a common strategy and to obtain from the company information about its future plans. Arrangements for discussion on production and employment exist between the Philips company management and Continental unions. The Dunlop-Pirelli unions have decided to set up a world council, to negotiate internationally and to obtain information about programmes for the 210 factories, which employ about 178,000.

There is now an organisation representing unions based on the EEC and the EFTA, which, in an enlarged community, will represent about 30 million workers and will be in a powerful position to influence Community policies. The employers have their own European organisation, Union des Industries de la Commaunauté Européenne (UNICE), which brings together employers associations from the EEC member states and the Confederation of British Industry. There is also an organisation which represents the Chambers of Commerce of the EEC and the applicant countries — the Permanent Conference of the Chambers of Commerce and Industry of the EEC.

2

International Comparisons

Any observer of the economic and social scene in the ten countries which will form the enlarged Community, will be struck by the differences which exist not only between the Four and the Six, but within the Six themselves. There are differences in size, geography, population and in political and economic institutions — though all the countries are parliamentary democracies. Within each country, there are regional differences, in terms of standards of living and employment, most marked in Italy, France and the United Kingdom. In the fields of labour relations, collective bargaining, trade union organisation and social security, there are widely differing systems, which have developed as a result of historical, cultural and national traditions.

There is no intention, and there never has been, of imposing any universal social legislation on Community countries. This would clearly be undesirable, even if it were possible. The Commission, however, has the broad aim of promoting some degree of coordination and harmonisation of social systems, in order to raise the standards of all who live in the Community.

A series of tables in this chapter illustrates the divergencies which exist in different economic and social areas, where these lend themselves to tabulation.

Tables 2.1 to 2.3 show the demographic and economic characteristics of the Ten − population size and densities, gross national product size and growth, and employment analyses by occupational status and main economic sector.

The annual average increase in GNP in the Six during the 1960s (Figure 2.2) ranged from 3.4 per cent in Luxembourg (heavily dependent on slow-growth heavy industry) to 5.8 per cent in France. Within the Four, the growth rate in the UK (2.8 per cent) was the lowest of the Ten, and the average per capita income per employed person the lowest, apart from Ireland (1970).

Apart from Italy, with its under-developed southern region, the countries of the Six have not experienced unemployment problems. In 1958, the EEC unemployment rate was 3.4 per cent; by 1963 it had dropped to 1.4 per cent, rising to 2.3 per cent in the 1967 recession. In 1971, the annual rate was 1.8 per cent, compared with 3.6 per cent in the UK. In all the Ten countries, unemployment is essentially a regional problem, but in all the Six, with the exception of Italy, there has been a persistent shortage of labour and the gap has been filled by the recruitment of migrant workers.

Tables 2.4 and 2.5 examine the relative levels of wages and recent growth characteristics. It will be seen from Table 2.4 that labour costs are highest in Norway and Denmark, followed by Germany, and that those in the UK are relatively low in the scale. Wage rates have risen steeply in all the Ten countries, as have prices. In Germany, Italy and the Netherlands, the least prosperous of the Six in 1958, real wages have been rising at a rapid rate, bringing them into line with those of the other three members of the Community. In all Ten countries, there is deep concern about inflationary trends and about the need to adopt restraints. This problem is being dealt with by various means − fiscal policies, statutory intervention, and voluntary cooperation − but nowhere can the efforts be said to have produced satisfactory results. No EEC country has succeeded in combining full employment policies with cost stability. The Commission has suggested that Governments should aim to keep wage increases to a limit of 6-7 per cent per annum, and price increases to 3 per cent. There is, however, no suggestion of any EEC incomes policy emerging.

The Treaty of Rome provides for 'equal remuneration in the same work as between male and female', but, as shown in Table 2.5, there is still a wide gap between men's and women's earnings, ranging from 56 per cent in Luxembourg to 77 per cent in France. The gap is being progressively closed, by escalating the women's rate of increase in national agreements. As far as the UK is concerned, the Department of Employment points out:

'Comparisons between earnings in the UK and these (EEC) countries need to be regarded with great caution because of various differences in the basis of the statistics used, and in premium and bonus payments . . . Differences in overtime premia and shift premia, together with differences of definition, probably make it necessary to raise the UK percentage by several points in order to provide a reasonable basis for comparison with the other countries.' (Office of Manpower Economics, Equal Pay, 1972.)

Labour relations, in terms of working days lost through disputes (Table 2.6) vary considerably. The statistics show that Italy and Ireland had the worst records during the 1960s and Germany and the Netherlands the best. Britain's average losses of working days during the period 1961-70 were about the same as those of France (apart from 1968) but the UK 1971/2 strike figures have been the highest in any post-war year.

Labour relations cannot however be measured statistically – they depend so much on the existing economic situation, the organisation of the two sides of industry, methods of negotiation and imponderable human factors. Collective bargaining is everywhere accepted as the basic method of determining wages and conditions, as is the right of association (as laid down in ILO Conventions). Within the Six, and to some extent in Denmark, Norway and Ireland, bargaining tends to be carried on within a legal framework and agreements are frequently vested with the backing of the Law. In many of these countries, there is provision for a national minimum wage, on a statutory basis.

This legal framework which, in many cases, originated from the weakness of the workers' organisations, is accepted by the European trade unionists, whereas in Britain, the Industrial Relations Act, which would bring British practice more into line with that of the Six, has been opposed by the unions. On the Continent many agreements lay down specific procedures for conciliation and some (eg in Germany) prohibit resort to strikes during the currency of an agreement. In the UK, conciliation procedures are usually on a voluntary and mostly *ad hoc* basis, though in some industries there is recognised agreed machinery. In all the Ten countries, there is a growing tendency towards plant bargaining, to supplement national agreements or, in some cases, to replace them. In general, employers and union organisations prefer to settle their differences by direct negotiation, rather than through State intervention, but in most countries, there is machinery for State mediation and conciliation. Special arrangements are usually made for the protection of the lowest-paid workers, on the lines of the British Wages Councils.

Wage systems vary considerably, though there is a common tendency for workers in engineering, chemicals, oil and the new growth industries to be

13

at the top of the earnings table.

Perhaps the biggest differences within the Ten are found in the strength and structure of their trade union movements. Employers' organisations developed relatively late, and do not present much divergence in their patterns.

Only in Britain and Germany are the unions organised on non-sectarian lines, under a single co-ordinated central leadership, but there are wide differences between the British and the German movements. In the United Kingdom, where the trade union movement is the oldest and biggest of the Ten, the unions grew up piece-meal and present a patchwork picture, with a few very large organisations and a multiplicity of craft, and even, local bodies. Structural reform has proceeded slowly and there are still about 150 different unions. In Germany, by contrast, as a result of the sweeping post-war reconstruction the unions are centralised and organised in 16 groups, on an industrial basis.

In France and Italy, the unions are divided on political grounds and in both countries, the Communist-controlled groups are dominant. In Belgium, Luxembourg and the Netherlands, likewise, there are different organisations for Christian and Socialist workers, but in these countries, and also in Italy, there has been an increasing trend to submerge ideological differences and to present a common front in negotiations over wages and conditions.

Throughout Europe, the unions attach great importance to securing fringe and welfare benefits, and these benefits add considerably to labour costs. (See Table 2.7.)

The differences in philosophy are shown very clearly in the union attitudes towards workers' participation, and in their determination to ensure for their members a greater say in the conduct of their enterprise. In all countries, except the UK, Italy, Denmark and Norway, legislation has been passed to provide for workers' participation. Works Councils machinery has been developed most strongly in Germany, where recent revisions of the 'Mitbestimmung' (cooperation) laws give the members of the councils increased rights vis-à-vis the management. Many European countries provide for statutory and/or negotiated protection against dismissal for members of works councils (see Annex, p.203). Although Britain was a pioneer in joint industrial cooperation, through the Whitley Council machinery set up after the first World War, the trade unions do not appear to give high priority to this issue, and the TUC is not in favour of legislation.

The length of working hours and holidays is determined either by legislation or by collective agreement, backed by legislation. Holidays are longer in all the EEC countries and in Norway and Denmark than in the UK and Ireland. In France, the legal minimum is 4 weeks, with eight-ten public holidays and supplementary holidays in some industries according to age and length of service. In the UK, the basic entitlement is two, sometimes three weeks, with six public holidays.

The length of the working week is fairly standardised at about 42½ to 45 hours, though in many EEC countries, the 40-hour week is the established legal standard. Most overtime payments are on the basis of 25 per cent on the basic hourly rate for the first two hours and 25 per cent beyond these, (UK $33\frac{1}{3}$ per cent for the first two hours, and in Norway 40 per cent for the first two hours).

In every country of the enlarged Community, there is a comprehensive system of social security, which has developed according to the differing social and economic conditions. The process of harmonising social security policies has not developed very far, and there are wide differences in principle and practice. All countries, however, recognise the major fields in which people need protection (sickness, old age, disability, industrial accident, family allowances, unemployment etc) and in all, the insurance principle prevails. The accounts given in subsequent chapters show the wide divergencies between the various schemes. Most EEC countries adopt earnings-related contributions and benefits. The UK system is still based on the flat-rate principle, although an element of earnings-related benefit has recently been introduced. There are differences in rates of contribution and benefits in the various countries, and in methods of administering and financing the schemes (see Table 2.9).

Among the differences, the following points may be noted: in respect of family allowances, the age limit ranges from 15 in UK to 18 in Germany and Italy, and 19 in Luxembourg; in Germany and the UK, allowances are not paid in respect of the first child. In all countries, payments are continued beyond the limit if the child is studying or disabled.

None of the EEC countries operate a comprehensive National Health Service on the lines of the British system. In many cases, the insured person has to pay his own medical fees, and recoup 75-80 per cent of the cost from sickness fund. In Germany, Italy and the Netherlands, he may have to make a contribution towards medical and hospital costs.

Although in all six countries, old age pensions are linked to the cost of living index, the rates of contribution and benefits vary widely. In the Netherlands, as in the UK, there is a flat-rate pension. In many countries, the existing pension is supplemented through collective bargaining. In some countries of the Six, private funds for pensions have been established on a

15

company basis.

As Table 2.9 shows, a heavy burden for social insurance payments falls on employers in the EEC, particularly in France and Italy. In all six countries, expenditure on various forms of social security has risen sharply and adjustments are constantly being made.

Tables 2.10 and 2.11 indicate some of the differences in living standards and prices. It is impossible to compare living standards, and to quantify these, as tastes and customs vary so widely. The French and the Italians eat more grains, fruit and vegetables and drink more wine than the British who, in their turn, drink more milk and eat more potatoes. The Belgians, Germans and Irish are the biggest potato-eaters and the Norwegians and the Danes consume the most milk and dairy produce. The list of differences is inexhaustible, though in all countries, there is a tendency away from starchy foods towards meat and other higher-grade produce.

Other difficulties in assessing living standards are the variations in individual incomes in different jobs, regions and industries; the problem of the rate of exchange; and the differing levels of taxation and social benefits.

But two generalisations can be made. One is that the standard of living in all the EEC countries has risen rapidly in the past 15 years, and in Italy and the Netherlands is beginning to catch up with that of the other members. Another generalisation is that the cost of living in EEC countries is extremely high, measured in British terms, especially in the price of foods.

Rents and house property are probably about as high in London as in Bonn and Paris, and higher than in Amsterdam or Brussels, though in all countries prices are lower outside the capital. The Department of Employment's Family Expenditure Survey (June 1972) shows that in the UK next to food, which accounted for 25.9 per cent of average household expenditure, and transport (13.7 per cent) housing came third in the list at 12.8 per cent.

Another indicator of living standards is provided by the consumption of consumer durable goods (Table 2.10). This shows that Luxembourg and France came first and second in car ownership per thousand population, Britain and Germany first and second in the number of TV sets and Denmark, Luxembourg and Norway were the first three in the number of telephones.

Housing is still perhaps the major problem in nearly all the countries of the enlarged Community, which all have a backlog of derelict and obsolescent houses to replace. Building progress is shown in Table 2.12. It indicates that Germany spends the largest proportion of its GNP on house-building (7 per cent) and that in 1970, most houses per thousand inhabitants were built by Denmark, Norway, France and the Netherlands (in that order).

Public health has improved throughout Europe as a result of higher standards and the increased attention paid to preventive medicine. At the end of 1969, Italy had most doctors per 100,000 inhabitants (179) followed by Germany (154.5). Ireland, Luxembourg and Norway provided most hospital beds per 100,000 inhabitants (1,308, 1,265 and 1,186 respectively).

Harmonisation of taxation systems is not specifically mentioned in the Treaty of Rome, but it is clearly an issue of concern. As shown in Figures 2.13 and 2.14, the rate of personal taxation varies widely between Italy and France, where it is low and the high-tax countries of Scandinavia and the UK. In Denmark and the UK, a higher proportion of revenue is derived from indirect taxation than in the Six. The EEC countries have adopted the method of Value Added Tax, but the rates and the items covered vary widely. Standard rates of VAT range from 11 per cent in Germany to 23.46 per cent in France. The UK is introducing VAT in March 1973, probably at a flat rate of 10 per cent for most goods and services, with certain exceptions (eg zero rating for food, books and newspapers) and exemptions for insurance, education and funeral services.

A final Table (2.15) indicates the differences in remuneration of typical senior management executives in EEC countries.

It is obviously not possible, in a brief chapter, to do more than provide general signposts to living costs and standards in various European countries. Much detailed information can be obtained from the various publications and organisations listed in the Appendix.

	Total population		Population density (1970)
	1970	Projection 1980	per sq. km.
	millions	millions	
Belgium	9.69	10.15	318
France	50.77	54.80	93
Germany	61.51	62.50	248
Italy	54.46	58.40	181
Luxembourg	0.34	0.35	131
Netherlands	13.00	14.46	356
UK	55.71	59.55	228
Denmark	4.92	5.30	114
Norway	3.88	4.30	12
Ireland	2.94	3.33	42

TABLE 2.1 Population — size and density

	1970 (£ million)	% of Ten
Germany	77,700	28.3
France	61,500	22.4
UK	50,600	18.5
Italy	38,800	14.2
Netherlands	13,000	4.8
Belgium	10,700	3.9
Luxembourg	8,400	3.1
Denmark	6,500	2.4
Norway	4,800	1.8
Ireland	1,600	0.6

FIGURE 2.2   Gross National Product — size and growth

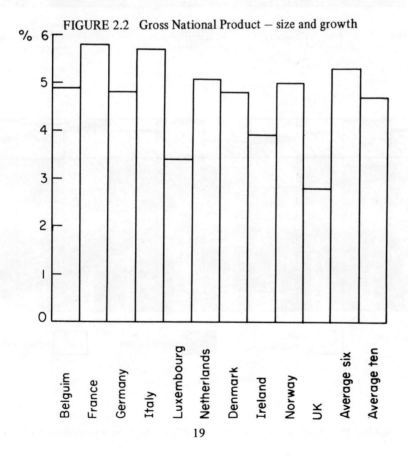

19

MAIN SECTORS

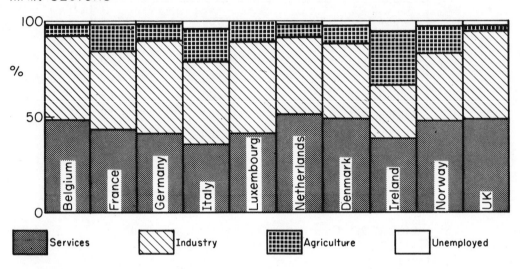

Services Industry Agriculture Unemployed

OCCUPATIONAL STATUS

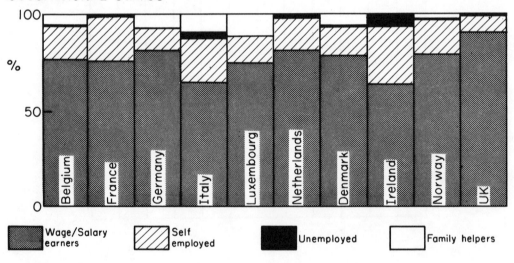

Wage/Salary earners Self employed Unemployed Family helpers

FIGURE 2.3 Employment Analyses by Main Sector and Occupational Status

20

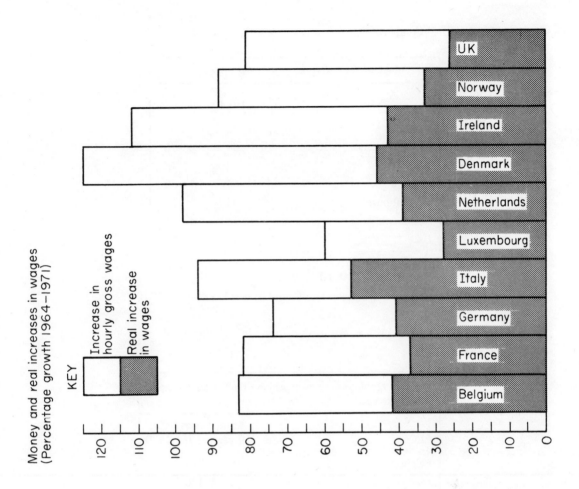

Money and real increases in wages
(Percentage growth 1964–1971)

KEY

Increase in hourly gross wages

Real increase in wages

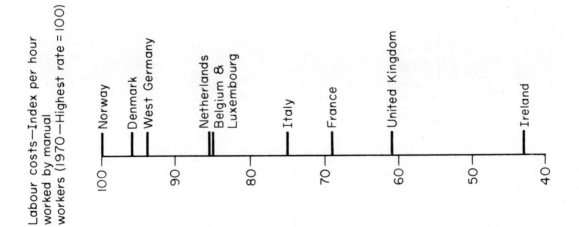

Labour costs—Index per hour worked by manual workers (1970—Highest rate = 100)

FIGURE 2.4   Labour Costs and Wages Growth

International Comparisons

Percentage of male average hourly earnings		
	1964	1971
France	76	77
West Germany	69	70
Italy	70	76
Belgium	65	68
Luxembourg	45	56
Netherlands	56	61
UK	57	59

Source: EEC, ILO, DE Gazette

Office of Manpower Economics, Equal Pay, August 1972

TABLE 2.5 Women's earnings in manufacturing

Per '000 employees in mining, manufacturing, transport and construction [1]	
EEC	Annual average for 10 years. 1961-1970
Belgium	226
France	306
West Germany	23
Italy	1,093
Netherlands	25
Denmark	414
Ireland	1,049
Norway	115
United Kingdom	321

Source: ILO, DE Gazette

TABLE 2.6 Days lost through industrial disputes [2]

[1] Methods used for collecting statistics vary from country to country.
[2] Estimated at 15,300 owing to industrial disturbances of May 1968

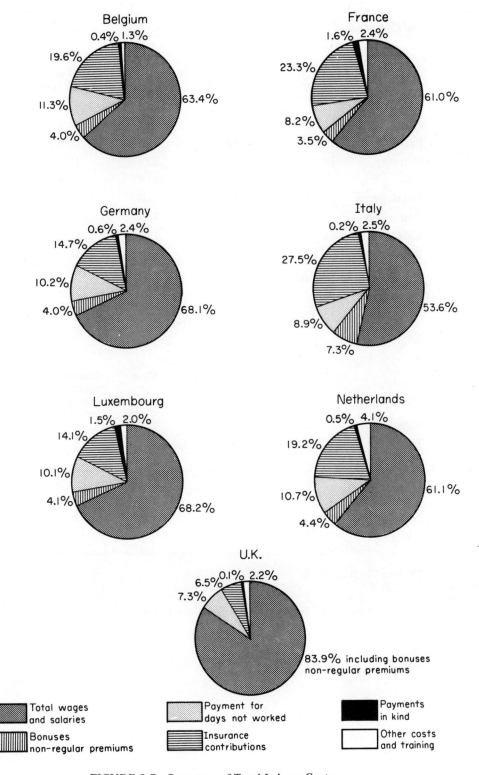

FIGURE 2.7 Structure of Total Labour Costs

	Total £ m	% increase over 1962	Expenditure per headof population £	Total as a % age of GNP
Belgium	1,725	138	178	16.1
France	9,840	168	194	16.0
Germany	13,350	124	217	17.2
Italy	6,435	196	118	16.6
Luxembourg	60	104	180	16.5
Netherlands	2,485	243	190	19.1
UK (1970-1)*	6,530	122	118	15.2
Ireland (1969)	155	123	53	10.5

* Public expenditure only

Sources : EEC, CSO

TABLE 2.8 National expenditure on Social Security

	Employer	Insured person	State	Interest on capital and other receipts
Belgium	53	23	20	4
France	68	23	7	2
Germany	54	30	14	2
Italy	63	15	15	7
Luxembourg	40	23	28	9
Netherlands	47	39	6	8
UK (1968-9)	20	22	58	

Sources : ECSO, OECD.

TABLE 2.9 Sources of Social Security Finance

Numbers in use per 1,000 population

	Cars 1971	TV sets 1970	Telephones
Belgium	215	207	200
France	245	201	161
Germany	234	262	212
Italy	187	170	160
Luxembourg	267	183	311
Netherlands	200	207	242
The Six	220	216	185
UK	213	284	253
Norway	193	207	283
Denmark	219	250	328
Ireland	122	153	98
The Ten	218	231	203

Source: EEC, OECD, Quoted in Common Market and Common Man, June 1972

TABLE 2.10   Comparative Standards of Living-Incidence of Selected Durable Goods

Expressed in £p	Belgium	Denmark	France	Germany	Holland	Italy	Norway	United Kingdom
Average rent for office accommodation per square metre	16.60	28.00	60.00	25.00	18.00	15.50	19.00	62.00
1 Kg best steak	1.93	4.44	2.63	2.35	2.89	2.13	3.45	1.98
10 fresh eggs	0.26	0.34	0.30	0.30	0.29	0.33	0.34	0.24
1 litre cooking oil	0.36	0.28	0.30	0.53	0.72	0.52	1.25	0.38
1 Kg sugar	0.14	0.16	0.14	0.14	0.16	0.17	0.11	0.10
1 large loaf	0.12	0.29	0.08	0.29	0.14	0.17	0.13	0.10
1 litre milk	0.08	0.09	0.08	0.09	0.09	0.11	0.09	0.08
2 Kg potatoes	0.09	0.12	0.12	0.15	0.08	0.09	0.14	0.05
Men's lounge suit	48.24	33.50	52.63	23.00	48.19	28.00	40.00	35.00
Men's shoes	8.77	9.71	10.53	8.15	8.43	7.56	6.72	9.00
Summer dress	17.54	13.87	12.03	7.35	10.84	11.52	11.68	11.50
Women's shoes	7.02	6.93	8.27	7.67	6.02	6.58	7.89	7.00
1 litre petrol	0.09	0.08	0.09	0.07	0.09	0.10	0.09	0.08
1 bottle whisky	2.63	3.88	2.26	1.88	2.11	1.64	4.32	2.65
1 packet cigarettes	0.18	0.43	0.26	0.24	0.21	0.28	0.37	0.30

TABLE 2.11 Comparative living costs 1972

Source: CBI 1972

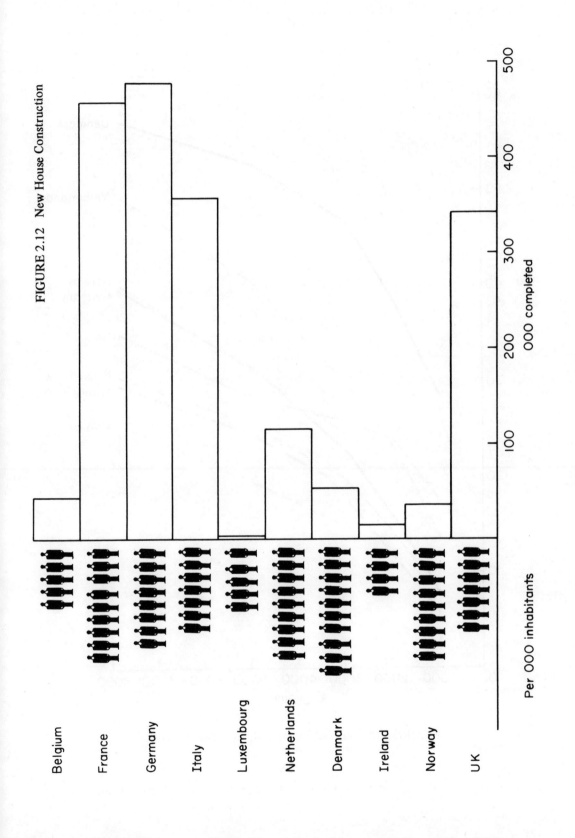

FIGURE 2.12 New House Construction

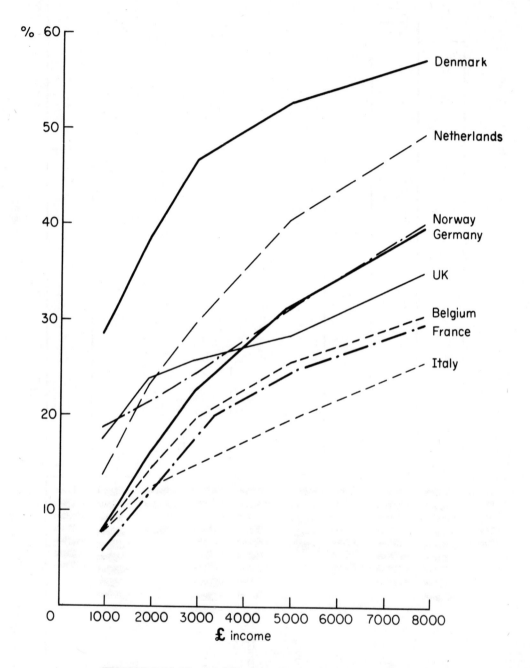

FIGURE 2.13 Personal Taxation Rates — Single Person

28

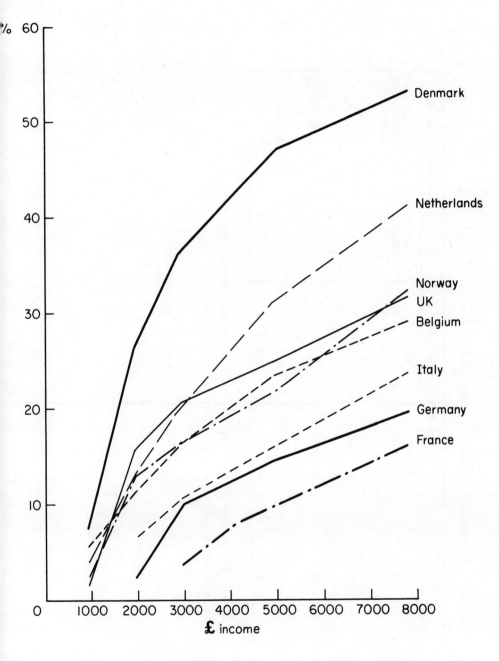

FIGURE 2.14 Personal Taxation Rates – Married with Two Children

29

Company with sales £21,000,000 – £42,000,000 p.a. 1969-70

	Chief Marketing Executive		Top Personnel Executive	
	Total gross remuneration	After Social Security and Income tax	Total gross remuneration	After Social Security and Income tax
Belgium	£14,350	£ 8,140	£ 6,460	£ 4,450
France	£17,540	£12,180	£ 7,020	£ 5,535
Germany	£17,080	£10,280	£ 7,000	£ 4,980
Italy	£15,650	£ 9,255	£ 7,155	£ 4,785
Netherlands	£13,050	£ 6,175	£ 5,875	£ 3,640
United Kingdom	£13,830	£ 6,855	£ 5,355	£ 3,785

Source: Top Management Remuneration Europe 1970. Management Centre Europe.
Based on Survey of 883 companies in 8 countries of Europe.

TABLE 2.15   Executives' remuneration

Part Two

The Six

Part Two

The Six

3

Belgium

GENERAL

With 9,690,991 inhabitants (1970) crowded into just under 30,500 sq.km Belgium has one òf the highest densities of population of the world (318 to the square km). Having common frontiers with the Netherlands, Germany, Luxembourg and France, it has become the natural focal point for Common Market activities and its capital Brussels, is the EEC's headquarters.

Despite its small size, Belgium's population is not homogeneous. About 55 per cent of the population are Flemish or Dutch speaking and inhabit the northern part of the country (West and East Flanders, Antwerp, Limburg and North Brabant). About a third, the Walloons, speak French and live in the southern half (Hainaut, Liege, Luxembourg, Namur and South Brabant). There is a tiny German-speaking group in Eupen-Malmedy, near the German border. Brussels, which lies in Flemish country, is officially bilingual, but its inhabitants are predominantly French-speaking. The Flemings tend to be conservative and Catholic, while the Walloons lean towards socialism.

There are traditional divisions between the two ethnic groups, mainly on religious, linguistic and cultural lines, but there are also economic problems. Flanders, with access to estuaries and the coast, has attracted the lion's share of industry, but the Flemings are conscious of the preponderance of the French in the economic life of Brussels.

The Walloons consider that the southern part of the country has been neglected in economic development. Following the constitutional reforms of 1970, which gave each community cultural autonomy — a step which might be regarded as a first move towards federation — tension has abated. It is important, however, that settlers in Belgium should be aware of the differences between the two sectors.

Belgium's gross national product was £12,200 million in 1971 (40 per cent of GDP from industry and 5 per cent from agriculture). It rose by 5 per cent in 1970 and the growth rate showed no signs of diminishing in 1971. Industrial production increased by 11 per cent in 1969 and 7-8 per cent in 1970.

The principal industries are iron and steel, non-ferrous metals, textiles, mechanical engineering, shipbuilding, chemicals, diamonds and glass. There is no indigenous car manufacture, but many American and European firms have established assembly plants. Oil refining increased fourfold in a decade, from 8.5 million tons in 1960 to 33 million tons in 1970 and is expected to increase to 46 million tons by 1975. Agriculture, though declining, still plays an important part and provides the Belgians with about 80 per cent of their food.

Belgium has no natural resources, apart from coal, and purchases its raw materials abroad.

Its main sources of imports are EEC countries, headed by Germany, with France and Holland taking second and third place. The same three countries occupy the same order in the export field. In all, exports from Belgium and Luxembourg to the EEC countries represent nearly 70 per cent of their total exports. Trade with the United Kingdom has declined. Pre-war, Britain took nearly 15 per cent of Belgium's exports, but in 1970 the share was only 3.6 per cent. The decline in British imports has been matched by exports and in 1971, the United Kingdom took only 6.2 per cent of Belgium's imports.

About 90 per cent of Belgian exports are in manufactured goods. The breakdown of imports and exports in 1970 was as shown in Table 3.1.

Belgium is a constitutional monarchy and the sovereign is Head of State. Executive power is vested in the Cabinet, under the Prime Minister. There is a two-chamber Parliament, with a Chamber of Deputies of 212 members, elected by universal suffrage on the basis of proportional representation and a Senate of 178 members, in which the 9 provinces are represented.

There are three main political parties: Christian Social (PSC), Socialist (BSP) and the Party of Liberty and Progress (formerly Liberal, PLP). In January 1972, the PSC and the BSP formed a coalition Government under the Premiership of a Christian Socialist.

Belgium is a free enterprise, competitive economy and the idea of State intervention is not acceptable. But there are some industrial spheres in which

Percent by Value			
Exports		*Imports*	
Non precious metals	28.1	Non precious metals	15.3
Textiles materials and		Machinery	14.1
manufactures	11.2	Minerals	13.3
Transport material	11.0	Transport material	11.6
Machinery	10.1	Textile materials and	
Chemicals	7.8	manufactures	8.6
Diamonds, precious stones	4.5	Diamonds, precious stones	3.8
Other goods	27.3	Other goods	33.3

Source: *The Belgian Economy,* Belgian Embassy, 1972.

TABLE 3.1   Analysis of Foreign Trade

the Government has been obliged to act, eg in regional development and in the introduction of concessions to stimulate investment. Until 1960 the country was cushioned by revenues from the Congo, but with the loss of its wealth-producing colony, Belgium had to take measures to strengthen its internal economy. To offset the losses, the Government offered incentives to attract both domestic and foreign investors, such as interest subsidies, or capital grants and various forms of tax reliefs.

As a result of these concessions and a number of other factors, Belgium offers an attractive proposition for foreign investment.

The excellence of communications in this small and compact country, its geographical position, the quality of its labour force, and the importance of Brussels as a financial and international centre can all be named as factors which encourage investment. During the 1960s over 4,000 foreign firms established themselves in Belgium, and American investment more than trebled. The principal firms to set up subsidiaries are in the chemicals, oil, brewing and vehicle industries.

Internal communications are by rail, road and canal. There are 4,165km of railways and 12,000km of trunk roads, including 520km of motorways.

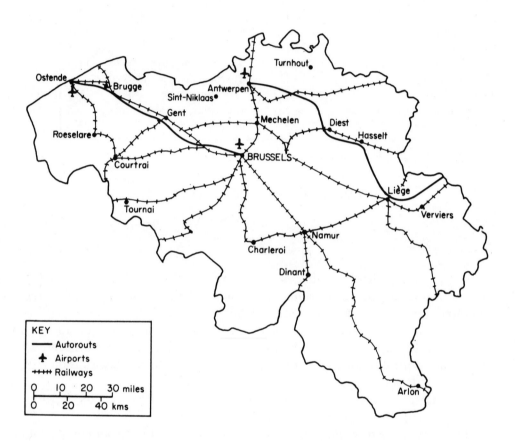

FIGURE 3.2 Major Centres and Communications

The network of canals, used for cargo freight, extends over 1,560km and links with the waterway networks of all the neighbouring countries. Belgium has a small but very modern merchant marine with over one million gross register tonnage.

Brussels airport, Zaventhem, 30 minutes by road and linked with the capital by a fast train service, is used by all international airlines. Sabena and BEA run frequent daily flights between Brussels and London, as well as flights to other British centres. Rail and sea connections to the United Kingdom ports are extensive.

MANPOWER RESOURCES

The total labour force was put at 3,918,100 in 1970, about one-third being women. Of the total, 45 per cent work in industry and 49 per cent in the services, and agriculture accounts for only six per cent. The great majority of male workers are engaged in manufacturing industry, while more women work in services. Coal, at one time the source of national wealth, now employs only two per cent of the working population.

	Male	Female
Metal manufacture and primary conversion	113,000	4,300
Manufacture of metal goods	71,900	13,600
Manufacture of non-electrical machinery	62,900	6,600
Electronic machines and equipment	54,400	25,500
Transport industry	92,000	7,400
Miscellaneous manufacturing	20,700	4,200
All manufacturing	824,600	273,100

Source: EEC

TABLE 3.3   Analysis of Employment in Manufacturing Industry 1969

In 1971 2.9 per cent of the working population were unemployed, compared with 2.7 per cent in 1963 and 4.5 per cent in 1968.

As in all EEC countries, Belgium has been admitting foreign workers. There are about 600,000 foreigners in the country, excluding workers from EEC countries, with the exception of Italians who number 175,000. The Spanish are the biggest non-EEC group, with 49,000, followed by Moroccans, 21,000, Greeks, 14,000 and Turks, 11,500. There are also Portuguese, Yugoslavs, Algerians and Tunisians, and a small number of Congolese nationals. Owing to the tendency to reserve the more skilled jobs for Belgian and EEC nationals, other migrant workers tend to take up semi or unskilled jobs in declining or unattractive work. They are found in coal-mining, domestic service, transport and general service trades, or working as labourers in construction and engineering. Most of them settle in the industrialised urban areas. The Belgian Government has pursued a positive policy of integration, but, as everywhere in Europe, the immigrants find themselves in an unfavourable position in respect to language, education and housing.

Increasing attention is being paid to the question of vocational and industrial training and re-training, whether for immigrants, the unemployed, people who wish to change their jobs, or for young workers. There is in Belgium a system of vocational schools, to which children can go after completing primary school at the age of 11. This is in two levels, catering for ages 12-14 and 15-17, but, as many children leave school before completing the upper level course, they do not receive adequate initial job-training, and have no opportunity to move to the higher technical and vocational schools for the age of 18 and over. To help to meet the problem of the young unskilled workers, the Government passed a series of laws in the 1960s, requiring employers to allow workers between 16 and 26 to attend training schools during working hours and without loss of pay.

There is relatively little apprenticeship training in the larger industries, though it is usual in crafts, trades and small and medium-sized firms. It is normally for a four year period.

On-the-job training tends to be informal, though a number of industries, eg textiles, and coal-mining, are developing more systematic programmes. The National Employment Office, under the Ministry of Labour, provides training and re-training at Government workshop centres for adults, which cater primarily for unemployed workers and those wishing to upgrade their skills. It also makes grants to employers who provide suitable re-training schemes for workers affected by production changes.

Unemployment is a problem in South Belgium, as a result of the decline in coal-mining. Owing to political and linguistic difficulties, there is little mobility of labour between the south and the more prosperous north. The Government has therefore aimed to bring new industrial development to

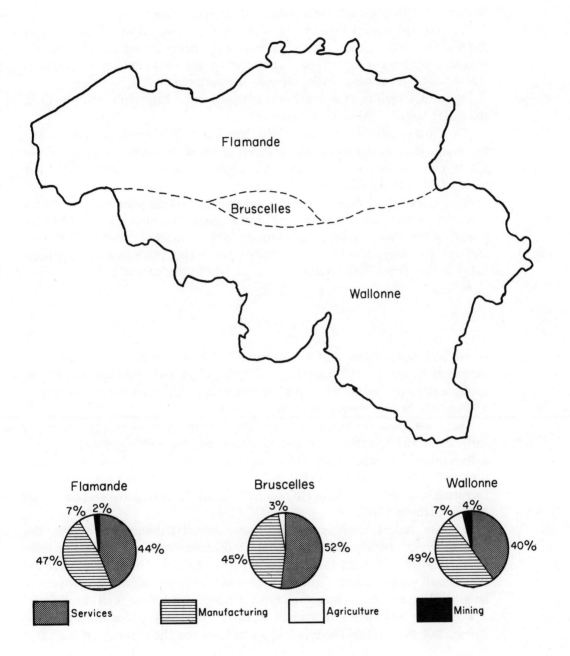

FIGURE 3.4   Employment Profiles by Region

Wallonia and thereby achieve a better balance in the economy.

The unemployment rate in the Walloon region stood at 3.3 per cent in 1968 − a rate very close to twice that which was being experienced in Brussels at that time (1.8 per cent). The corresponding rate for Flanders, the northern region, was 2.5 per cent − very close to the national average.

Figure 3.4 highlights the variations which exist between employment in the major sectors within each region.

The Government's regional efforts have met with some success. It was reported[*] that in the Borinage of which Mons is the centre, there are only 1,500 men employed in one coal-mine, compared with a total mining labour force of 30,000 in 1948.

A new industrial estate has been developed, making aluminium sections, glassware, telecommunications equipment, beer, pharmaceuticals and other goods, while many workers are finding jobs in machine tools, electronics and car assembly. Similar developments are taking place in the Liège area. Many British firms have established themselves in this part of Belgium.

WAGES

Wages and salaries have risen steeply in Belgium, though not to the same extent as in other EEC countries. Between 1958 and 1970 the real rise in wages was estimated to be 56 per cent, the consumer price index standing at 137 and the hourly gross wages index at 214.

There are great disparities in earnings. The ten highest groups for men's earnings in 1970 were: petroleum, coal mining, shipbuilding, iron and steel, automobiles, base chemicals, metal manufacturing, chemical products, transport and machine tools (in that order). Average hourly earnings for manufacturing were 59.54 Belgian (Bf) francs, and 62.22 in building and construction in October 1969.

A more recent analysis by the International Labour Office gives the breakdown of hourly rates in certain industries in Brussels and the main towns (Figure 3.5). With the exception of building craftsmen, rates were the same in all areas. Recent figures are also available for salaried employees in Belgium. Figure 3.6 sets out some typical monthly rates for such employees.

Equal pay for men and women work is obligatory under the Treaty of Rome, but in practice there is still a gap between the earnings of men and

---

[*] *The Times, 31st May 1972*

October 1971	Bf
Coalmining, face workers	111.60
Food manufacturing	72.00
Clothing, men's shirts	52.07
Furniture	77.10
Printing and publishing	78.16 - 84.79
Chemicals	52.25
Engineering (skilled)	66.93
(labourers)	53.55
Garage mechanics	65.75 - 82.85
Building, (tradesmen)	77.00
(labourers)	61.70
Electricians, (skilled)	81.75
(unskilled)	65.83
Railways, porters	49.79
Bus & Tram drivers	58.85 - 61.85
Lorry drivers	62.86
Municipal services	48.53

Source: ILO

FIGURE 3.5 Hourly Wage Rates in Selected Industries

October 1971	Bf
Laboratory assistants	9,705
Sales assistants (retail)	9,255
Clerks (Male)	9,255
Shorthand typists	10,197
Bank tellers	11,500
Bank machine operators	11,930 - 12,350

Source: ILO

FIGURE 3.6 Monthly Rates of Salaried Employees

41

women, and in manufacturing industry, women receive about 68 per cent of male earnings.

A table showing the relative position of European countries in relation to labour costs in 1971, is given on page 21. A more detailed, though less up-to-date, survey gives a breakdown of labour costs for each of the Six, and covers both manual workers and staff employees (Table 2.4). The variations which exist in incomes between regions are set out in Figure 3.7.

Wages are normally paid in cash, but, subject to the written consent of the employee, they can be paid through a post office, a bank or savings bank. Manual workers are usually paid fortnightly, and staff employees monthly.

Employers may find themselves paying out extra sums for particular purposes, eg especially dangerous or unhealthy work, night work, certain types of shift work, clothing, tools, travel and in respect of training expenses.

Working hours are being progressively reduced. Under a Law of 1964 the week was fixed at 45 hours, with the intention of reducing it to 42 in 1972/73, and to 40 hours in 1975/76, by collective agreement.

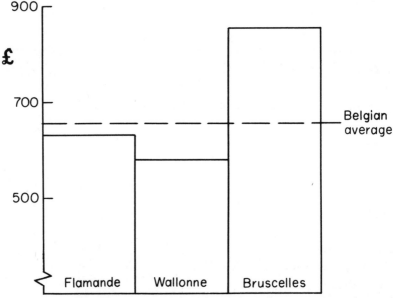

FIGURE 3.7   Average Incomes by Region

Overtime, above eight hours a day, is paid at 25 per cent on the basic hourly rate for two hours, and at 50 per cent thereafter. Double time is paid for Sunday, which is officially a day of rest. Actual hours worked in manufacturing industry (October 1970) were 42.6.

The Belgian worker is entitled to three weeks holiday on full pay, plus ten public holidays. (New Year, Easter Monday, May Day, Ascension Day, Whitmonday, National Day, Assumption Day, All Saints Day, Armistice Day and Christmas Day).

SOCIAL SECURITY

As in all EEC countries, Belgium has a comprehensive system of social security, covering sickness and disablement, unemployment, old age and death, family allowances, maternity, and occupational injuries and illness. The system is administered by the Office National de Securité Sociale in Brussels, but there are separate arrangements for seamen, miners and the self-employed. The system was extensively revised at the end of 1967, in order to unify social security arrangements by merging the separate schemes into a single one.

As shown on Table 2.9 (p. 24) the employer bears 50 per cent of the cost of financing social security, compared with 23 per cent from the employee and 27 per cent from the State. Social security expenditure accounted for 16 per cent of the GNP in 1970.

Both contributions and benefits are normally related to income and linked with the cost of living index. Salaried employees' contributions are lower than those of manual workers, and it is planned gradually to raise these to the same level. The worker's contribution amounts to 10.55 per cent of his earnings and that of a salaried employee to 8.55 per cent.

Sickness and Disablement

All employees are compulsorily insured, and the scheme is administered by mutual funds and sickness societies. The employer pays 3.75 per cent of a monthly earnings ceiling of Bf 26,075 towards medical benefits and 1.80 per cent towards cash benefits, up to a ceiling of Bf 15,775. Wage earners and salaried employees, rates are 2 per cent towards medical benefits. The wage earner pays 1.20 per cent towards cash benefits, and the salaried employee 0.80 per cent.

Medical benefits include general medical and specialist treatment, hospitalisation and supply of medicines, but the insured worker bears not more than 25 per cent of the expenses. Treatment in the case of such diseases as cancer and tuberculosis is free. Cash allowances, to compensate for loss of earnings, are paid after the third day. They amount to 60 per cent of the earnings ceiling for temporary disability (up to one year), 60 per cent for continued disability (up to two years), and 40 per cent for a further period of two years. Manual workers receive 80 per cent of their wages during the first week of sickness. In all cases there are maxima.

Workmen's compensation for industrial accidents has existed in Belgian Law since 1903 and applies to all insured workers. The employer is required to pay premiums for insurance which vary according to the risk of the occupation. The average amount is 3.7 per cent for workmen and 1 per cent for office employees, up to an annual earnings ceiling of Bf 306,000.

Benefits include medical treatment and cash allowances. For temporary incapacity, these amount to full pay for the first day, 90 per cent of average earnings for the second and third days, and 80 per cent for the remaining period of disablement, up to a ceiling of Bf 306,000 a year. In the case of permanent disablement, there is a pension up to 100 per cent of average daily earnings plus a constant attendance allowance (maximum 50 per cent).

Survivors' benefits include provision for widows, orphans, and other dependants. There is a lump sum death grant, equal to 30 times average daily earnings.

The same benefits are payable for occupational diseases. All employers are required to insure their workers through occupational disease funds. Contributions, paid for exclusively by the employer, amount to 0.65 per cent of the earnings ceiling for office employees and 0.75 per cent for manual workers.

Salaried workers are entitled to 100 per cent of their salary during the first month of incapacity.

There is a separate contribution for health services, the employer paying 2.65 per cent and the employee 3.10 per cent on earnings up to Bf 182,500 per annum.

An insured worker is considered disabled when his earning capacity is reduced to one-third of the normal standard for his grade. A pension will be paid at the end of the period covered by sickness insurance, ie three years, or when he is classified as permanently disabled. It is at the rate of 60 per cent of the earnings ceiling for an insured person with dependants, and 40 per cent of that for one without dependants.

Retirement & Other Pensions

Contributions are paid jointly by employer and employee. Table 3.8 sets out the basis of these contributions.

Per Cent	Office Employees			Manual Workers		
	Employer	Employee	Total	Employer	Employee	Total
	7.25	5.00	12.15	8.00	6.00	14.00
1972	7.50	5.25	12.75			
1973	7.75	5.50	13.25		No change	
1974	8.00	5.75	13.75			
1975	8.00	6.00	14.00			

Source: Social Insurance News, April 1972, Assicurazioni Generali, Trieste.

TABLE 3.8 Pension Contributions

The present salary ceiling Bf 18.450 a month will apply from 1974 to wage earners as well.

The ceiling and the amount of pension are linked with the retai¹ price index.

Everybody, including foreign nationals employed in Belgium is eligible for a State old age pension. The pension is normally paid at 65 for men and 60 for women, but there is provision for earlier retirement on a reduced pension.

Pensions, for a full working life of 45 years for men and 40 for women, equal 60 per cent of average annual career earnings. For a married couple, where the wife is not working or is entitled to a pension in her own right, the pension is increased to 75 per cent. The maxima are Bf 95,000 for a single person, and Bf 113,000 for a married couple.

Survivors' benefits are paid to widows, at a rate equal to 80 per cent of her late husband's accrued or actual pension, provided she is over 45, or two-thirds incapacitated or caring for a child. Otherwise she will receive a lump sum equal to one year's pension. Orphans' allowances are paid as part of family allowances at a flat rate of Bf 1,929 per child plus supplement according to age.

Full tax relief is granted on contributions, but the old age pension itself is subject to tax. There is an annual State subsidy.

Many Belgian companies operate private pension schemes, usually for the benefit of salaried employees and higher paid staff, particularly those whose earnings exceed the State plan's ceiling. These schemes are usually on a contributory basis. More than half the plans of leading companies are based on final pay, ie either the average salary of the last three years *or* the salary of the year before retirement. Benefits usually amount to 60-70 per cent of final pay, including State pensions after a full career. The figure of 50 per cent is normal for top management. The schemes normally provide widows and orphans benefits. They are financed by direct insurance, by company-administered funds and by book reserves or internal company funds. There is full tax relief on contributions towards an approved private pension plan.

Family & Maternity Allowances

Belgium was the first country to introduce family allowances. The scheme is paid for entirely by the employer and amounts to 10.50 per cent of the earnings ceiling to Bf 185,400 a year. Allowances, which start at the first child, are at the rate of 650 francs a month for the first, 1,100 francs for the second and 1,500 francs for the third and subsequent children. The normal age limit is 16. There is also a system of birth allowances.

Maternity benefits comprise medical benefits on the same basis as that provided for sickness, and cash benefits for a period of 14 weeks. This equals 60 per cent of the earnings ceiling. An allowance of 100 per cent of the earnings ceiling, paid entirely by the employer, is provided for the first seven days for manual workers and for the first 30 days in respect of office workers.

Unemployment Benefit

All employed persons under 65 are covered. Contributions are divided between the employer, who pays 1.70 per cent of the earnings ceiling, and the employee who pays 1.20 per cent. There is one waiting day and benefit is of unlimited duration. Maxima are Bf 226.57 a day (single) and Bf 246.44 (married). The amount varies according to age, sex, place of residence and marital status, and is conditional upon the recipient being able and willing to work and being registered with the Office National de l'Emploi. This office plays a positive role in stimulating employers to take on unemployed men, by paying a certain percentage of wages and helping with their resettlement and training.

LABOUR RELATIONS AND PROCEDURES

Recruitment and Contract of Employment

Engagement of workers is done mainly through Government bureaux, and Government-subsidised private employment agencies, which are not allowed to charge fees, except in the case of domestic workers, performers and artists and agricultural workers. Both types of agency come under the control of the Ministry of Employment and Labour's National Employment Office (a semi-public body administered by a Board of Governors with joint management-labour representation). For recruiting staff and executive personnel, many employers advertise in local or specialist newspapers, and use the services of management consultants for engaging top management personnel.

Every employer is required to maintain a register of all personnel, giving information about each worker's identity and civil status, his job, insurance coverage and dates of beginning and terminating employment. There is also an individual employee record, which covers social security arrangements. The compilation of such records involves a mass of paper work, so many firms hand over the job to special offices, called 'Social secretariats'. These were established in 1945 and come under the jurisdiction of the Ministry of Social Welfare and the National Social Security Office.

Once a worker has been hired, there follows a complex procedure of drawing up the contract. There are five categories of contract, covering apprentices, merchant sailors, manual workers, white collar workers and sales representatives. The two most important are the work contract for manual workers and the employment contract for non manual workers. The work contract usually provides for a trial period, of from seven to fourteen days, followed by a written or verbal contract of unlimited duration, unless a worker is engaged for a specified time or duty. To terminate a contract, an employer must give in writing at least fourteen days' notice, although the length of notice is increased according to length of service. An employer is obliged to give workers time off (up to one day a week) to find new employment.

The contract for salaried workers is on the same basis, but the trial period ranges from one to three months and longer notice of termination is stipulated (a minimum of three months for up to five years' service and progressively increased).

The employer does not have to give reasons for dismissing an employee, but if he fails to observe the legal notice period, he will have to indemnify the employee. Termination notices may not be given during annual vacation close-down, or because of military service, or if a woman is pregnant.

Collective Bargaining

As in Britain, collective bargaining is voluntary and does not rest on an explicit legal basis. But the system has in fact become so well-established that it has virtually acquired the force of law.

At national level, there is a National Labour Council, set up in 1952 and representing the two sides of industry. It has both advisory and executive functions. It advises the Government on general social and labour matters and, since 1968, has been empowered to conclude collective agreements, for example on supplementary holidays, productivity policies and the provision of information to works councils. It has been described as 'a kind of social Parliament enacting general rules that apply to the whole private sector of the economy' (International Labour Review, July–August, 1971).

Until the mid-1950s, the Government took a hand in wage settlements, but now responsibility for industry-wide agreements lies with joint industrial committees, representing both sides of industry. These committees have three main functions: to conclude collective agreements, to provide conciliation for the settlement of disputes and to give general advice to the Government, the National Labour Council and other bodies. The councils fix legally binding minimum wages, decide on job classification, and deal with general conditions of employment, working conditions and apprentice training.

Collective agreements usually run for two years, and are linked to the retail price index. Although they vary in complexity, they contain certain common features, eg guarantees for union representation, pay categories according to skill and age, arrangements for bonuses, hours, holidays, overtime, training, shift work and procedures for settling grievances and disputes. Non union workers benefit from the general provisions of the contracts. Salaried workers are dealt with by separate machinery. Most supervisory personnel negotiate individually with employers.

Most industrial agreements provide for basic grades according to skill. For example the construction industry distinguishes four categories: non-qualified, specialised, and two grades of skilled labour, with fairly wide differentials between the categories. Young workers are paid according to a percentage age scale, reaching adult level at 21.

Over and above the minima set by the JICs, negotiations at plant level often provide for considerable increases. In the chemical industry, for example, plant-level bargaining is far more important than that at national level.

In May 1960, management and labour organisations agreed on a system known as 'Social Programming'. Its main principle is that the worker should be entitled to increases in his standard of living made possible by the growth in national wealth. This aim, it was recognised, must be realised through industry-level collective bargaining and can only be achieved if industrial peace is preserved during the currency of the collective agreement. In consequence, most agreements contain a 'no-strike' clause, and stipulate that all procedures must be exhausted before there is recourse to industrial action.

Procedures for settling disputes are not defined in legislation and although Labour Courts exist, there is in practice very little reference to arbitration.

An industrial worker with a grievance will seek redress through his union 'délégation' (equivalent of 'shop stewards') and if no settlement is reached, the matter will be referred to regional officials. Failing agreement, at enterprise or regional level, a dispute will go through the conciliation procedures of the joint industrial committees. The Ministry of Labour has a body of mediators, who are available to help in the settlement of disputes.

The Belgian workers are less strike-prone than their neighbours in France, though more so than the Dutch. As the Table on p. 00 shows, they came fourth in the 'League' table of fewness of days lost through strikes in the 1960s. The right to strike is guaranteed by law, but on the whole union leaders tend to regard industrial action as a last resort. Most strikes are usually of short duration, and the most frequent cause is pay. During the 1970s, there was a rash of unofficial strikes at plant level, many of which broke the 'peace' clause of the social programming agreements.

Trade Unions and Employers

Labour is highly organised in Belgium and about 65 per cent of all workers belong to unions. In the most important sectors of industry, including metal-working, chemicals, cement, petroleum and mines, the proportion is almost 90 per cent. Among white collar workers, the figure is only about 40 per cent.

The trade union movement is divided on religious lines. The two most important bodies are the Confederation of Christian Trade Unions (CSC) with over one million members and the Socialist-inclined Belgian General Federation of Labour (FGTB) with 823,379 members. There is a smaller

Federation of Liberal Unions, with 120,864 members.

Workers are mainly organised on an industrial basis. Employers negotiate with the 'most representative trade union organisation' at national, industrial and plant levels. This means in practice the Christian and the Socialist bodies.

At plant level, unions are represented by 'délégations', who are either elected or appointed, and have general shop steward functions. They enjoy almost complete security of employment.

The most important employers' organisation is the Federation of Belgian Industries (FIB). Most Belgian employers, including Belgian subsidiaries of foreign firms, are affiliated to it through some 50 industry-wide federations, covering every aspect of industrial life.

The Belgian Federation of Non-Industrial Enterprises (FENIS) looks after the interests of insurance companies and banks. There is also an organisation for Flemish employers. Together the FIB and FENIS represent management as 'social partners' in various joint and/or tripartite committees, such as the National Labour Council and the Central Economic Council, semi-Government National Boards and the joint industrial committees.

Works Councils

Works councils are legally obligatory in enterprises employing more than 150 people. They consist of equal numbers of management and workers' representatives, who are elected by secret ballot every four years. These councils meet at least once a month and usually follow model procedural rules drawn up by the industry's joint industrial committee.

They are consulted on such matters as hiring and firing policies, labour legislation, working rules and conditions, productivity, holidays and welfare. Under a collective agreement of December 1970, works councils are entitled to be informed and consulted before any decision is taken which will affect employment in the plant. They must be informed at least once a quarter about the financial and economic position of the company.

In all enterprises with more than 50 workers there are compulsory health and safety committees, which supervise the application of safety and health legislation. This legislation is very comprehensive. It provides for protection against accidents at work, including compulsory protective clothing, and lays down standards of ventilation, cloakroom, canteen etc facilities. A statutory occupational health service provides for physical examination of minors and workers exposed to the risk of industrial disease, and gives general advice on health and hygiene, and the fitness of workers to undertake particular jobs.

4

France

France is the largest country in Western Europe, covering an area of 551,200 square kilometres but with a population of just over 50 million. Its population density, 93 inhabitants to the square kilometre, is the lowest of the Six.

The postwar expansion of the French economy has been as spectacular and rapid as that of any of the Six. Large tracts of the country and entire cities were devastated during the War and it was only in 1948 that the national income caught up with the 1938 level. During the 1950s a new momentum developed which has continued unabated. In 1961 the Gross National Product (Market prices) was 328,327 million francs. It increased at an annual rate of 5.8 per cent between 1965 and 1970, by when it had more than doubled compared with the beginning of the decade.

This increase can be attributed to the continuing shift in the economy from agriculture to industry, and to the concentration on research, science and innovation in the industrial sector. The level of industrial production has steadily risen and is still rising. In March 1972, the index (1962 = 100) stood at 178.

Yet, although industry contributes seven times as much in value as agriculture to the national product, France is still, apart from Italy, the most

51

agriculture-oriented member of the original Six. Much of its industry and trade is based on the preparation and processing of the produce of its farms, market gardens, orchards and vineyards.

The industries with the fastest rate of growth are mechanical and electrical engineering, chemicals and petro-chemicals, while building and services have also expanded rapidly. Traditional industries like coal-mining have declined, as the French have progressively turned to other sources of energy. Textiles have lost ground to artificial fibres. Fashion and luxury trades and tourism are important sources of national wealth.

Natural resources, apart from rich soil in some regions, include coal, iron ore and potash. Plans for the accelerated exploitation of natural gas and water nuclear power are being pursued and prospecting for oil and uranium is being stepped up.

France is not a traditionally export-minded country. It has about a million major manufacturing enterprises, but only about 500 firms account for four-fifths of total sales abroad. Since the establishment of the EEC, there has been a big expansion of trade within the Six, notably with Germany which is now France's biggest single customer.

Its main exports are machinery, transport equipment, including cars, chemicals, iron and steel, mineral fuels, clothing and footwear, food products and alcoholic drinks. Its imports follow a similar pattern (apart from food and drinks).

France has been a Republic since 1870. Between the end of the Second World War and 1958, when General de Gaulle assumed power, there were no fewer than 26 different Cabinets. Executive power resides in the President, who is elected by direct universal suffrage for seven years, and a Council of Ministers, headed by the Prime Minister. In June 1969 M Georges Pompidou was elected President. Parliament consists of the National Assembly and the Senate, which is elected on a territorial basis.

France exercises a dominant voice in the counsels of the EEC. It was originally on French initiative, as a result of the efforts of MM Jean Monnet and Robert Schuman, that the first steps towards a Common Market were taken with the creation of the European Coal and Steel Community in 1950. France joined the EEC on its establishment in 1958 and by reasons of tradition, culture and experience, the French have frequently been able to influence its entire policies.

Although France is basically a free enterprise country, the Government plays an important role in steering economic development. It has adopted a series of five year national plans which lay down economic and social targets, and guidelines for their achievement. The sixth and latest plan (1971-75)

FIGURE 4.1 Major Centres and Communications

drawn up after consultation with a large number of interested organisations and individuals, goes into less specific detail than its predecessors, and lists 25 main objectives as priorities. The aim is a growth rate of 5.8 to 6 per cent per year, with annual rises in industrial production of about 7.5 per cent and of 7 per cent in productive investment. The main emphases are on improving the transport infrastructure, eg roads, ports and urban traffic, regional re-organisation, education, training, housing and the achievement of higher living standards.

There are no travel problems for British executives and visitors. The main British and French national air lines BEA and AIR FRANCE operate regular and frequent flights between London and Paris, as well as flights from Birmingham, Glasgow, Manchester and Bristol, and serve most of the main French towns.

There are also flights operated by independent airlines. There are abundant train and cross-Channel car ferry services, including hovercraft, and a network of railways, most of which begin and terminate in Paris.

The Government is proposing to spend many millions of francs during the next five years in building motorways, expanding internal waterways largely used for goods carriage, new airports for Paris and Lyon, modernisation of ports and railways.

France already has over 36,000km of railway lines and over 7,600km of inland waterways in use, with a fleet of 7,500 vessels. Its merchant navy consists of nearly 6,000 ships, half of which are tankers.

MANPOWER RESOURCES

France's total civilian labour force in 1970 was estimated to be 20,773,000 and was expected to increase at the rate of 0.9 per cent per year during the ensuing five years. The number of wage earners and salary earners in 1970 was 15,882,000, compared with 13,003,000 in 1960. Of this, industry accounted for 7,929,000 and agriculture, fishing and forestry for 2,865,000. Comparative figures for 1960 were 7,070,000 and 4,193,000 for industry and agriculture respectively. Building in 1970 accounted for 2,089,100 and transport, service, commerce and other activities for 9,773,400 workers.

Unemployment has remained at a low rate, although it has increased over the last five years. The average for 1971 was 336,000. Some concern has been expressed about the provision of suitable jobs for young workers. As a result of the high postwar birthrate, there has been an influx of young people onto the labour market, averaging nearly 600,000 a year between

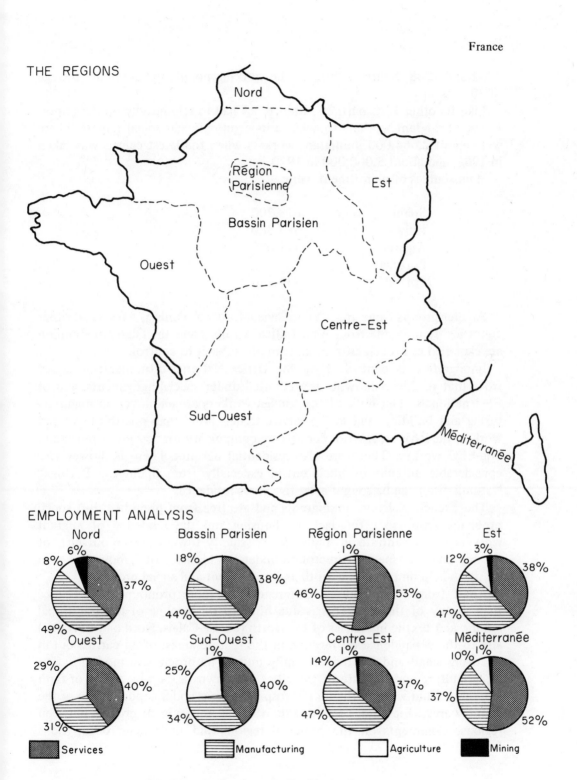

FIGURE 4.2   Employment Profiles by Region

1962 and 1968. Nearly a third of the working population are under the age of 30.

Like its other EEC partners, France has had to rely heavily on the importation of migrant workers to achieve its economic and social targets. There were about 2,664,000 immigrant workers when the latest census was taken in 1968, and about 3,000,000 in 1970.

Main sources of recruitment were:

Spain	618,200
Italy	585,880
Algeria	471,020
Portugal	303,160
Poland	131,280

Smaller groups came from Yugoslavia, Morocco, Tunisia, Africa and other countries. Immigrants from West Indian Antillais and the Island of Reunion are classified as French citizens and are not subject to control.

Immigration is controlled by the Office National d'Immigration, apart from that of Algerians who are recruited under special agreements, and of EEC nationals. The bulk of the foreign workers are employed in manufacturing and building, and in the service trades. More than one-third live and work in the Paris area. Work permits are compulsory for any non-French and non-EEC worker. There are also residential permits. There is, however, a considerable amount of illicit entry, especially from Spain and Portugal. Naturalisation can be sought after five years residence.

The French welcome immigrants and are free from prejudice. But social problems arise from the lack of housing and the tendency of migrant workers to concentrate in 'bidonvilles', (shanty towns) on the outskirts of the big cities. A special Directorate under the Ministry of Labour has been set up to help immigrants with their employment and social problems.

Apart from Italy, regional differences are more pronounced in France than in any of the Six. This is due both to the decline of the traditional mining and textile industries of the North (Pas-de-Calais, Nord and Lorraine) and to the dependence on farming in the remote areas, often carried out in relatively small and inefficient family units. The progressive modernisation of agriculture and the lure of the cities and towns is causing a drift of farm workers to find work in the more prosperous areas and a depopulation of the country areas. Figure 4.2 sets out the varying employment profiles between regions. Comments on the principal regions and their main occupations follow.

Region Parisienne Metal-working, vehicle manufacturing, electrical materials, food processing, as well as fashion and luxury trades and tourism. It contains nearly a fifth of France's total population and average wealth in the region is 30 per cent above the national average. The unemployment rate is below average.

Bassin Parisien Forms a wider zone surrounding the immediate Paris area and includes such centres as Cherbourg, Orleans and Reims. Agriculture plays a far more important role in this area and unemployment is marginally above average.

Nord Pas-de-Calais and Nord, has been heavily dependent on the declining coal mining and textile industries, although the employment balance has to some extent been redressed by metallurgical and engineering industries and increased activities in the Channel Ports. This region has a relatively small proportion of female employees.

Ouest Remains the area with the strongest element of employment in agriculture and fishing (29 per cent). The region covers the Brittany peninsular, in the north, to the Gironde estuary in the south. Average incomes compare poorly with the neighbouring Bassin Parisien region and with the national average.

Est Including Alsace and centred on Strasbourg, exploits iron ore and produces the great bulk of France's pig iron and steel output, together with glass, crockery and china, printing, motor cars and miscellaneous goods. Building materials, potash, coal, chemicals and fertilisers are important products. The area is also rich agriculturally.

Sud-Ouest Predominantly agricultural and wine-growing, has tended to be relatively neglected, but efforts have been made to introduce modern and consumer goods industries. The natural gas fields of Lacq are attracting producers of light alloys and metals. Shipbuilding and fishing are important activities. The region remains at present however an area of relatively high unemployment and low incomes.

Centre-Est With Lyon as the main centre, was formerly dependent on silks and textiles and is now additionally manufacturing steel, heavy engineering products and chemicals. Grenoble has become the centre of scientific and technological research. There is a rapidly developing sector in electronics, electrical engineering, hydraulics, chemicals and petro-chemicals. Locomotives and heavy machinery are produced at St Etienne. The triangle represented by Lyon-St Etienne-Grenoble is expected to become one of France's most important and fast-growing modern industrial regions.

Mediterranée The region includes both the south coastal zone of France and the island of Corsica. The coastal zone contains Marseille, France's leading port, with the important petroleum refinery interests round the Etang de Beurre and a wide diversity of manufacturing products. Fruit, vegetables and wine, and above all tourism are the principal activities in Provence and the Cote d'Azur.

In general, industry is scattered throughout France, and many smaller centres operate small-scale industries, in mainly agricultural areas.

The least developed and poorest areas are Brittany, Midi-Pyrenees, Poitou-Charentes and parts of the Mediterranean region, where there is above average unemployment and per capita income is only three-quarters of the national average.

The priority aims set out in the Sixth Plan include efforts to limit the growth of the Paris Region, to build new motorway-linked towns and to stimulate development in the backward regions, by improving the infrastructure and offering investment inducements. More modern industry will be 'steered' to traditional industrial areas such as the Nord, and Lorraine and it is hoped to create new jobs in the Massif Central, the West and South-West.

Another high priority in the Plan is vocational and industrial training and it is planned to double the number of post-school schemes by 1975, so that 1,700,000 people will receive vocational training. The emphasis is on training young people but schemes for adult workers (including older workers, women and migrants) are also being developed. The first Industrial Training Act, covering industry, agriculture, the civil service and management, was passed in October 1966 and a further Act in 1968 rationalised the system of trainees' wages. Employers and trade union organisations have reached a comprehensive agreement on vocational and refresher training. Training is one of the responsibilities of the Labour and Employment Directorate of the Ministry of Labour, Employment and Population; there is also a National Association for the Vocational Training of Adults (AFPAO) which, under the supervision of the Ministry, runs courses for adult workers. The adult schemes include part-time and evening classes, courses at technical institutions and special training centres, as well as extensive radio and TV programmes.

In July 1970 employers and union leaders reached a national agreement on the extension of training. It provided that young workers, up to the age of 18, should be enabled to attend courses during working hours, without loss of pay for up to 320 hours a year. Another section deals with the further training of redundant workers or those still in employment who want to take part-time or full-time courses.

In 1972 employers planned to devote 0.8 per cent of their total wage bills to financing occupational training, rising to 2 per cent in 1976.

WAGES

Both hourly gross earnings in industry and the consumer price index rose more rapidly and more steeply in France during the 1960s than in any EEC country except the Netherlands. Taking 1964 = 100, the earnings index stood at 182 in 1971 and (1963 = 100) the consumer price index at 133. The trend continued into the 1970s, with consumer prices rising at about 6 per cent per year and hourly wage rates estimated to be increasing at the rate of 10-11 per cent per year. Nevertheless, the French worker's rise in real wages has not been as steep as in other European countries. Estimated to be 37 per cent between 1958 and 1970, it was the lowest of any of the Six except Luxembourg (Table 2.4). This was partly due to the price inflation and partly to the emphasis laid by the trade unions on securing increases in fringe benefits.

Despite a rapid increase in output per man-hour, labour costs in France have been steadily rising. The break-down of these costs is shown in Table 2.7.

There is a wide disparity in gross hourly earnings. Among the lower paid groups, earning under five francs per hour, are included food manufacturing, clothing and footwear, leather and textiles. Higher-paid workers, in the six to nine francs range, include chemicals and plastics, metallic ore mining, printing and paper, engineering and petroleum (1969). A 'League' table shows that the top ten industries in October 1970 were printing and publishing, petroleum, metallic ore mining, preparation of metallic ores, base chemicals, glass, aircraft chemical products, automobiles and transport. Substantial variations exist in average incomes between regions. Figure 4.3 charts the situation in 1968 and highlights the very great difference which is apparent between incomes in the Paris area with the rest of France.

Despite the fact that France was the first country in West Europe to establish the principle of equal pay for men and women, and pressed for its

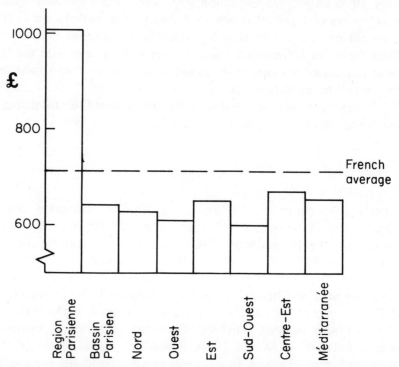

FIGURE 4.3 Average Incomes by Region

inclusion in the Treaty of Rome, there is still a gap in earnings, though it has recently been narrowing. In October 1970, women earned 76 per cent of men's earnings in miscellaneous manufacturing industries, 78 per cent in metal manufacture and 84 per cent in electrical machinery and equipment.

France was also the first country to introduce the forty-hour week, as one of the reforms of the pre-war Popular Front Government. This was re-affirmed in legislation in 1950, either on the basis of a five-day eight-hour week, or a six-day six-hour week. Yet average hours actually worked in manufacturing industry totalled 45 in October 1970, with as much as 49.3 hours for steel workers 44.5 in 1971. Overtime, up to a limit of 20 hours a week, is legally permitted, and is paid on the basis of a flat supplement of 25 per cent on the basic hourly rate for the first eight hours.

The French worker enjoys longer holidays than any European, apart from the Italian. Negotiated by collective agreement, paid annual leave is equal to two working days a month up to 24 workdays and eight to ten public holidays, in all 32-34 days a year. Holiday pay is negotiated by agreement — in engineering it amounts to one twelfth of total annual earnings.

SOCIAL SECURITY

The French workers attach as much importance to social security and fringe benefits as to money wages, and they have succeeded in securing progressive gains in this field. The employer bears the biggest share of the social security burden of any EEC country. (See Table 2.9). Apart from Italy, the cost of benefits in France, over and above wages costs, is the highest in any EEC country.

There are three main national insurance funds, dealing respectively with sickness, disability, death and industrial injury, old age and family allowances. There is an unemployment scheme, providing assistance in the form of flat rate benefits with a special compulsory scheme (UNEDIC) for industrial and commercial employees, providing wage-related benefits.

Contributions and benefits to Insurance funds, apart from unemployment assistance which is refunded by the State, are related to earnings.

On earnings up to Fr 19,800 a year, contributions are made on the basis set out in Table 4.4.

Per Cent	Employer	Employee	Total
Sickness, maternity, disability	10.45	2.50	15.95
Old age and survivors	5.75	3.00	8.75
Family allowances	10.50	-	10.50
Industrial injury and occupational disease (average)	3.00	-	3.00

Source: Social Insurance News, April 1972.

TABLE 4.4 Contributions to Social Security

On total earnings, sick pay contributions amount to 2 per cent from the employer and 1 per cent from the employee.

There is a series of special insurance schemes for miners, farm workers, seamen, civil servants and railwaymen.

Sickness and disablement

Insured persons are entitled to general medical and specialist treatment, hospitalisation and medicines, from the onset of illness. The patient usually pays the fees, but can recoup 75-80 per cent of the cost, or 100 per cent if the illness is serious or protracted. Daily cash allowances from the fourth day of sickness amount to 50 per cent of insurable earnings, of $66\frac{2}{3}$ per cent after the 31st day if there are three or more children. The allowance normally lasts for 12 months, but can be extended to three years if the illness is long drawn-out.

Pensions vary from 30 to 50 per cent of earnings according to the rate of disablement and the worker's earnings over the past 10 years, plus additions for constant attendance where needed.

Industrial injuries and occupational disease benefits paid for by the employer, distinguish between temporary and permanent disablement. In the first case, an injured worker receives a benefit of 50 per cent of insurable earnings, raised to $66\frac{2}{3}$ after 28 days, payable until recovery. In the latter case, there is a pension which varies according to the degree of disablement, up to a maximum of Fr 103,282.48 a year. Constant attendance allowance, of up to 40 per cent of the pension, is paid where necessary. There are survivors' and funeral benefits. An employee is entitled to medical treatment during the period of disablement.

There are strict regulations enforcing safety and health at work, very much on the lines of the British system. All enterprises must establish their own works medical service, or join an inter-factory service. The employer covers the costs, including the pay of a works doctor, who carries out regular medical inspections, and generally supervises health and hygiene arrangements.

Retirement and other pensions

Pensions are payable at the age of 60, but are usually deferred to 65. At 60 the pension amounts to 20 per cent of average annual earnings in the ten years before retirement; at the age of 65, it is 40 per cent with a maximum of £553.84 per annum. The pension is increased by 10 per cent if the recipient has brought up three children.

For non-manual, supervisory, technical and executive staffs, there is a special compulsory insurance scheme, financed by employee and employer contributions and administered according to a somewhat complex principle known as 'repartition'. This is the distribution of current contribution income among people who are entitled to benefits, without accumulation of funds.

Contributions are converted into 'pension points' and credited to the employee and the value of the pension point is fixed periodically. Benefits are based on the number of points credited to the employee on his retirement. This scheme was first established by collective agreement in 1947 and was incorporated in the Labour Code in 1960.

Administration is in the hands of 'caisses' (of which there are about 150) supervised by three central bodies.

There is a special optional scheme for higher-paid persons (cadres superieurs).

Because of the high cost of these schemes to the employer, there is less scope for the development of private pension arrangements than in some countries, but many of the larger companies in fact supplement the legal benefits with private arrangements.

The State scheme provides for suvivors' benefits. These are paid to widows or dependent widowers, on the basis of 50 per cent of the pension at the time of death or of his/her entitlement, if the survivor is under 60. If the survivor is 65 and over, or 60 if incapacitated there is a minimum pension of Fr 1750, with 10 per cent more if there are three children of under 16. Orphans' pensions are payable as part of family allowances. Survivors are entitled to a funeral grant based on the deceased persons earnings.

Family and maternity allowances

Family allowances are paid monthly. If there is only one wage-earner, the first child is entitled to receive Fr 38.90 allowance otherwise the benefits are on a progressive scale — Fr 38-90 for the second, Fr 97-25 for the third and subsequent children. The normal maximum age is 16½.

Insured women receive medical treatment and cash allowances on the same terms as the daily sickness allowances for a period of 14 weeks (six weeks before and eight weeks after confinement). There are also pre-natal allowances, a maternity grant, plus a nursing allowance and milk vouchers for a period of four months.

Unemployment benefit

Compulsory for all employed persons under 65. There are two schemes, one of which is statutory and the other the result of collective agreements. In the statutory scheme, which is 100 per cent State-financed, flat-rate benefits amount to Fr 7.75 a day for the first three months and Fr 7.05 thereafter, (subject to a means test). There are additions for dependants (Fr 3.05) and a

10 per cent reduction in benefit after each year up to three years. In the collective agreement scheme (UNEDIC) benefits amount to 50 per cent of insurable earnings, during the first three months, and 35 per cent thereafter, plus dependants allowances, with a minimum of Fr 9.43 for the first 91 days and Fr 8.20 thereafter. Benefits last for 12 months or more according to age.

In 1963 the Government set up a National Employment Fund to help workers who are affected by technological change, provide re-training, and protect them against disturbances arising from new production methods. The Fund is the responsibility of the Ministry of Labour.

LABOUR RELATIONS AND PROCEDURES

The Labour and Employment Directorate of the Ministry of Labour, Employment and Population is responsible for labour affairs, including employment, training, labour relations and conditions of work. It has a network of local and regional offices.

Recruitment and contract of employment

The National Employment Agency is the main body for placing workers, though the services of independent bodies are also used. An employer is officially expected to notify the authorities of the number of workers he is engaging and to keep a register. He is also expected to employ a proportion of war disabled and give preference to fathers and widows with children to support.

For terminating a work contract he must notify the departmental manpower service within 24 hours and in the case of collective dismissals, must get the authorisation of a Labour Inspector, after consultation with members of his Enterprise committee.

Collective bargaining

There is not the same long-standing tradition of industry-wide collective bargaining in France as there is in Britain. The system was first developed during the lifetime of the Popular Front Government in the 1930s, with the so-called Matignon Agreement, but the present legal framework was only established under an Act of 1950. This provided for a minimum wage and equal pay and re-established the forty-hour week. The wage is adjusted according to changes in the retail price index.

Within the 1950 framework, a number of collective agreements have been negotiated, normally for a particular industry or 'occupation'. Sometimes these agreements are supplemented by local or regional agreements, as in textiles and metal-working. Bargaining at plant level has not progressed as far as in the United Kingdom, but it has become increasingly favoured by the trade unions, which see in them a means of gaining extra concessions. Since national agreements usually lay down minimum pay scales, the workers at factory level can bring pressure to bear on individual employers to improve their offers.

Usually the period of a national agreement is for one year, with the possibility of extending it.

All agreements contain some provision for conciliation, but they do not, as in Scandinavia, preclude strike action during the lifetime of the agreement. The State machinery for mediation and arbitration is rarely invoked.

The French Government often takes a hand in stimulating collective bargaining. It was on the initiative of the Pompidou Government that, following the unrest of May 1968, employers and union leaders produced the so-called 'Grenelle' declaration. This provided for an extension in the scope of collective bargaining, which now covers, (as well as wages, hours and conditions) holidays, union rights, training and employment policies, the position of women and young people, settlement of disputes, salaried status and profit-sharing. Nationalised industries and the civil service were brought into the ambit of collective bargaining.

Agreements have been concluded on job security, training, salaried status and profit-sharing. In June 1971, the Labour Code was amended to allow wage-earners to receive their pay monthly instead of fortnightly and to enjoy the same social advantages as salaried workers. These advantages include guaranteed incomes, seniority bonuses, longer notice and payment of additional compensation for dismissal. By May 1971, 39 such agreements had been reached in metal-working, building, chemicals, coal mining and elsewhere. It is expected that all wage-earners will be on the monthly system by 1975.

As for profit-sharing, a Government decree of 1967 makes it compulsory for firms with more than 100 wage-earners to give their workers a share in the benefits of industrial expansion and to establish special funds for this purpose. It is expected that about two million workers will eventually be affected. Each year, the firm sets aside a portion of its taxable profits in a special worker participation reserve, which is then allocated among the workers in proportion to their wage or salary. Nobody can receive more than 4,560 francs a year. The reserve is either distributed in the form of company shares, put into an investment fund, or paid to outside investment firms or into personal savings accounts within the firm. No payments can be made for a period of five years, though exceptions can be made in the case of illness, dismissal or death. The sums paid into the special reserve are exempt from profits tax.

The system, which is in keeping with the paternalistic attitude of many French employers, is designed to increase the worker's sense of identity and cooperation with the firm's interests.

Trade unions and employers

The French trade union movement is fragmented and split along political and religious lines. The three main centres are:

Confédération Générale du Travail (CGT), Communist-dominated, with 1¼ to 1½ million members in 41 affiliates.
Confédération Française Democratique du Travail (CFDT), the former Federation of Christian Workers, a socialist organisation with about 600,000 members.
Confédération Générale du Travail – Force Ouvrière (CGT-FO), anti-Communist, with its main strength in white-collar groups. Membership about 500,000.

Less important, numerically, are the Confédération des Travaileurs Chreitiens (CFTC) whose 100,000 members retain the Christian connection, and the Confédération Générale des Cadres (Executive and white-collar staffs) with 200,000 members. The teachers have their own organisation, the Confédération de l'Education Nationale, with about 400,000 members.

Because of its divisive nature, the trade union movement's membership has remained low and probably represents only about 20-25 per cent of the labour force. Political divisions have eroded its effectiveness and made the tasks of organising and collective bargaining more difficult. In general, the CGT tends to set the pace, and has never hesitated to resort to strike action, for political as much as industrial purposes. Recently however there have been signs of growing militancy on the part of CFDT.

Between 1961 and 1970 there was an average annual loss of 306 days per 1,000 workers in mining, manufacturing, transport and construction (this excludes the May 1968 unrest). Because of a lack of solid foundations and funds, there is a preference for the short-term, or lightning strike and the use of go-slow tactics. Wild-cat strikes are frequent.

Employers by contrast, are more effectively organised in the Conseil National du Patronat Francais (CNPF), which has about 150 affiliated trade associations and three major federations. Its functions are mainly co-ordinating and limited to guiding the individual organisations in general, although recently the CNPF has been taking a more direct part in negotiations.

Despite the Communist domination of the CGT and the strike-proneness of its members, relations between the two sides of industry have been improving, largely as a result of the 'Grenelle' statement, and typified by the use of the phrase 'social partners'.

Both sides of industry are represented on a tripartite Economic and Social Council, which gives advice on labour legislation and regulations. They are also regularly consulted on the drawing up of the National Plans.

In general, the French system of labour relations embodies an extent of legal activity, which would not be tolerated in Britain. This is largely due to the weakness of the trade union movement, and the need for the Government and the Law to provide the fullest protection. The whole system is codified in the comprehensive 'Code du Travail'.

Works councils

At plant level, in every concern where more than 50 workers are employed, there are legally-backed works councils (Comités d'entreprise). The number of worker representatives varies according to the total numbers employed. Elections take place every two years and members represent the various categories of workers. The council must be consulted on such matters as working rules, codes of discipline, employment and training, redundancies, and must be kept informed of the firm's financial status and prospects. Employers must allow the workers' elected representatives time off for meetings.

In addition, there are a number of hygiene and safety committees, which may be sub-committees of the enterprise committee.

Workers 'delegates', the equivalent of the British shop stewards, are elected annually. Their function is to present grievances to management and in general look after the interests of the workers at shop floor level.

5

Federal Republic of Germany

GENERAL

West Germany is the most highly industrialised, prosperous and technologically sophisticated country in Europe. It has the largest population of the EEC, with 61½ million people, including West Berlin, inhabiting a territory covering about 250,000sq.km at a density of 248 to the sq.km.

The Federal Republic is the leading industrial power in Europe. Its economy advanced very rapidly after the end of the War, when its shattered industries were rebuilt, modernised and rationalised. Recovery was greatly helped by aid under the Marshall Plan. The economy is still expanding, though at a slower rate than before. The gross national product was £77,300 million in 1970, compared with £34,000 million in 1960. This is the highest GNP figure for any European country. The annual rate of growth during the 1960s was of the order of 6 per cent.

Germany's national wealth derives from its strong industrial basis, although more than half the territory is classified as farmland and nearly one third consists of woods and forests. Yet agriculture accounts for only about 3 per cent of the gross domestic product, compared with 54.8 per cent for manufacturing.

The most important industries are iron and steel, mechanical and electrical engineering, vehicle building and chemicals, paper, optical goods, textiles and food. Employment in coal-mining has steadily declined.

The share of coal as a source of primary power is only half that of oil, which accounts for 54.4 per cent of the total; natural gas has been rapidly expanding.

Industry is highly concentrated. The main areas are the Ruhr, the Rhine-Main (Frankfurt), the Southwest (Stuttgart) and the Northeast (Hanover). The northern coastal region is becoming increasily industrialised.

The most remarkable postwar industrial developments have come in southern Germany, in the province of Baden-Württemberg, of which Stuttgart is the capital. New type activities such as electronics, aircraft, scientific instruments and nuclear research have emerged and new forms of energy and raw materials have been exploited.

Germany exports about one-fifth of its total production, 85.8 per cent being in manufactured goods. It imports manufactured and semi-manufactured goods, food and raw materials. It has had a balance of trade surplus since the mid-1950s. In 1970 the Federal Republic came second in world trade to the United States.

Its main export markets are EEC countries, headed by France and the Netherlands, the USA, EFTA countries and Britain. EEC and EFTA countries supply about 60 per cent of its imports. Chief exports in value, are non-electrical machinery, motor vehicles, chemicals, electrical machinery, iron and steel, textiles and yarn fabrics, precision instruments, optical and photo-mechanical products, coal, coke and briquettes. Chief imports are farm and food products, non-ferrous metals and semi-manufactured goods, crude oil and natural gas, and engineering products. In 1970, imports totalled 109,600 million DM and exports 125,300 million DM.

Between 1962 and 1970, production per employee increased by 52 per cent.

The West Germans attribute their economic success mainly to the fact that the economy is based on free competition. The Government's role is limited to 'steering' and setting the climate for expansion. Foreign investment is welcomed and at the end of 1970 totalled £2,460 million.

Politically West Germany is a federal republic with a democratic constitution (adopted in 1949). Basic rights, enforceable under the law, guarantee individual freedom and the right to participate in every aspect of society. The chief legislative organ is the Bundestag, with 518 members elected by direct universal suffrage. The Head of State is the Federal President, elected for a period of five years.

The Upper House (Bundesrat) is made up of representatives from the ten

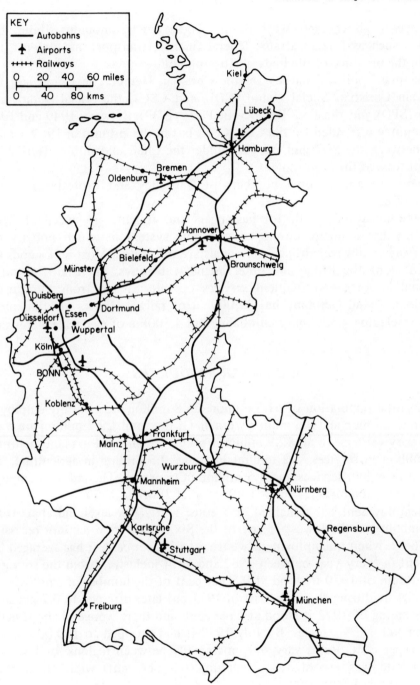

FIGURE 5.1   Major Centres and Communications

provinces (Länder) and West Berlin. These are autonomous States, but matters such as foreign affairs, federal finance, transport and defence fall within the province of the Federal Government.

The main political parties are the Christian Democratic Union and the Bavarian Christian Social Union (CDU and CSU), the Social Democratic Party (SPD) and the Free Democratic Party (FDP). Between 1949 and 1969 the country was ruled by the CDU/CSU, but in the autumn of 1969 a coalition between the SDP and the FDP under the Chancellorship of Herr Willy Brandt formed the Government.

There are about equal numbers of Catholics and Protestants in the population.

Communications, both for passengers and freight, are excellent. West Germany has a highly developed transport system in which policies for motorways, railways, airlines and canals are integrated. Most bulk goods are carried along the Rhine and other inland waterways. There are ten international airports and frequent services operate to and from the United Kingdom. In all Germany has 34,000km of railway track, 415,000km of roads, including 4,500km of autobahns and 4,500km of navigable waterways.

MANPOWER RESOURCES

Of the total population of 61.5 million, 26.8 million are gainfully employed 17.2 million men and 9.6 million women. Of the total, 22.2 million are wage and salary earners. In all 12.9 million workers are engaged in manufacturing, 4.5 million in services, 3.2 million in trade, 2.5 million in agriculture, 2.2 million in public services and 1.5 million in transport. The index of employment in manufacturing (1963 = 100) stood at 106.7 in 1970.

Unemployment has remained at a consistently low level and apart from Luxembourg, is the lowest of any of the Six. Apart from a minor recession in 1966-7, when unemployment went up to 2.1 per cent, it has averaged 0.7 per cent in every year between 1962 and 1971 inclusive. From the spring to the autumn of 1970 it stood at 0.5 per cent of the number of employed. It rose slightly during the early part of 1971 but later dropped to 0.7 per cent. In the spring of 1972 it stood at 1 per cent, and there were still about half a million unfilled vacancies. By July 1972 it had dropped to 190,000 or less than 1 per cent. Rates vary only marginally between regions. In 1968 the lowest rate was recorded in Hamburg (0.3 per cent) while the highest (Saarland) was 1.5 per cent.

Unlike France and Italy, West Germany has suffered relatively little from

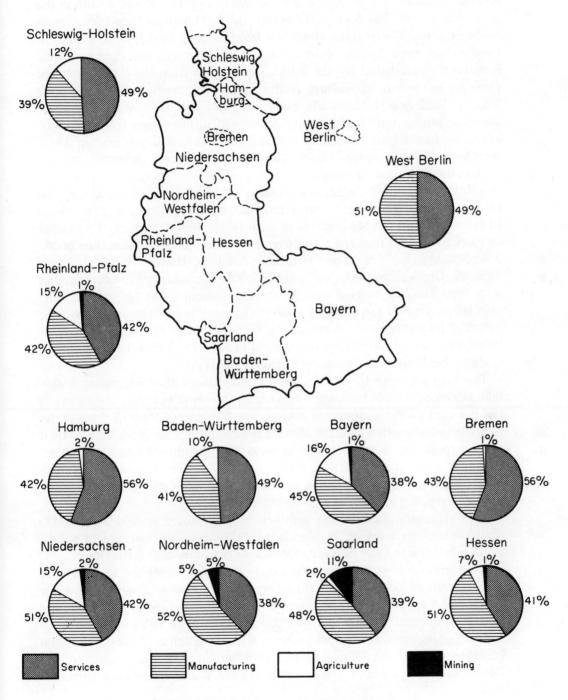

FIGURE 5.2 Employment Profiles by Region

regional imbalance. The rapid rise in national employment and wealth in the past twenty years has been fairly evenly spread. There are, however, certain problem areas. The regions along the frontier with East Germany have to some extent been by-passed by economic development and their problems have been exacerbated by the influx of refugees from the East. There are some regions where agriculture predominates, for example Bavaria, Lower Saxony, Schleswig-Holstein and parts of the Rhineland-Palatinate. In these areas the proportion of people engaged in agriculture ranges from 12 to 16 per cent, (see Figure 5.2). The national figure was 8.8 per cent in 1970. Another problem is caused by the run-down of traditional industries, such as coal, in the Ruhr and Saar regions.

Shortage of labour has been a constant source of concern to industry. To fill the gap — workers have been recruited, largely from Italy and from non-EEC countries in the Mediterranean area. In the past ten years, the number of foreign workers rose from just over 500,000 to 2.250 million. The breakdown in March 1971 was: Yugoslavs 436,000; Italians 388,000; Turks 385,000; Greeks 256,000; Spaniards 175,000; Portuguese 51,000. Together with their families, foreign workers represent about 6 per cent of the total population. One in ten workers in West Germany is a foreigner. The average length of their stay has been increasing. While Germany relies very heavily on its migrant labour, the Chancellor warned in June 1972 that the country was reaching the limit of the numbers it could employ.

The migrants tend to work in the less attractive industries and to undertake labouring jobs in building, engineering, transport and the public services (94 per cent of the dustmen in Munich are foreigners). Most of them prefer to settle in the south where the climate and conditions are more akin to their home experience than in the urban areas of the Ruhr-Rhineland. They get the same wages and conditions, protection and social insurance rights (including pensions) as the Germans but face social, educational and linguistic problems which put them at a disadvantage.

It is estimated that in the summer of 1972 there were about 18,000 British nationals working in Germany. Authorities do not expect a substantial increase in their number, owing mainly to language difficulties.

The Germans have become increasingly concerned with the need to build up the levels of skill, to match the advance in technology. Responsibility for training and apprenticeship is shared by the Federal Ministry of Labour and Social Affairs and the Ministry of Economics. In June 1969 a law on vocational training consolidated all previous legislation and established a Federal Institute for Vocational Training. The main burden of training, however, falls on industry and a major drive to improve the standard has been launched.

The programme includes industrial and safety training, and language courses for the migrant workers. Every year, about 1.15 million apprentices and young workers are trained for their chosen industry or trade.

The basic educational system is becoming increasingly geared towards meeting the needs of industry. There are schools giving specialised instruction in 50 different branches, including building, mechanical engineering, electronics, mining and textiles. Both the employers and trade union organisations play a constructive part in encouraging training and education. Towards the end of the 1960s, nearly one-third of the courses supplied in higher education institutes consisted of technological subjects.

Management training is primarily given within companies and most executives are recruited from the universities and technical high schools. A four-year course for managers was opened in Frankfurt in October 1971, but it was expected to be patronised mainly by smaller firms.

1971 DM	Minimum rates*	Average hourly earnings
Coalmining, face	6.14	8.20
Food manufacture	4.63 - 4.84	5.57
Clothing, men's shirts	-	(f)5.42 - (m)6.99
Furniture	5.30 - 5.95	5.86 - 7.38
Printing and publishing	5.36 - 7.66	6.69 - 9.06
Chemicals	5.06 - 6.00	6.47 - 8.38
Engineering (skilled)	4.63 - 6.35	7.75
(labourers)	4.04	6.16
Garage mechanics	5.05	-
Building (tradesmen)	6.10 - 6.70	8.21
(labourers)	6.12	6.60
Electricians (skilled)	6.61	8.14
(unskilled)	5.15	6.82
Railways, unskilled	5.57	-
Bus and tram drivers	5.80 - 6.10	-
Lorry drivers	4.30	-
Municipal services	4.53	-

* Minimum in highest seniority class and wage zone

Source: ILO.

TABLE 5.3 Wage Rates and Earnings in Selected Industries

WAGES

Owing to the shortage of manpower and to the strength of the trade unions, earnings have been pushed up steadily and increased in real value by 70 per cent during the 1960s. Taking 1960 as 100, the index of average gross monthly earnings in 1970 was 221.7, compared with a price index of 130.3.

Because of the orderly system of collective bargaining, the disparities in wages between different occupations are less than in many EEC countries.

Latest available figures, for 1971, show that weekly earnings averaged 302 DM, the figure for men being 327 DM and for women 209 DM.

A recent EEC Statistical Survey (1969) showed that average gross hourly earnings in manufacturing industry were 5.52 DM. The 'top ten' groups of industries in terms of earnings were (October 1970) printing and publishing, chemical products, petroleum products, automobiles, iron and steel, metallic ore mining, coal mining, transport, metal manufacturing and base chemicals.

A more recent analysis by the ILO gives the breakdown for selected occupations in October 1971 (Table 5.3).

Between 1962 and 1968 the wage/salary bill per worker increased by 53 per cent. Typical monthly rates are set out in Table 5.4.

Average Monthly Rates	DM
Laboratory assistants	1,262
Distribution	
Sales assistants (retail)	860
Clerks (male)	855
Shorthand typists (female)	765
Bank tellers	1,466
Bank machine operators	1,199

Source: ILO

TABLE 5.4   Earnings of Selected Salary Employees

Incomes differ greatly between regions. The results of an EEC enquiry, relating to 1968, are set out in Figure 5.5. This illustration shows that the Hamburg and Bremen areas enjoy high average incomes while in contrast three regions with strong agricultural communities — Schleswig-Holstein, Niedersachsen and Rheinland Pfalz — experience rates well below average.

The average weekly hours worked in non-agricultural occupations (excluding commerce and transport) during 1971 were 43.2, with 43 hours in manufacturing. There is strong union pressure for the further reduction of hours. Overtime in engineering is paid at 25 per cent of the basic hourly rate, including performance supplement, for the first two hours and at 50 per cent beyond that. Sunday is a rest day, apart from essential transport and maintenance operations.

The German worker is legally entitled to a minimum of 15-18 days holiday a year, but this is usually increased through collective bargaining to 16-24 days. In addition, there are 10-13 public holidays, making the total annual leave 25-37 days. There are additional days in some industries under collective agreements according to age and length of service.

SOCIAL SECURITY

Germany has a highly developed and long-established system of social insurance, dating back to the 1880s. The present system is administered by a variety of institutions, ie old age insurance by Länder institutes, sickness and maternity insurance by local, company or trade funds, and unemployment and family allowances by the Federal Labour Office. As shown in

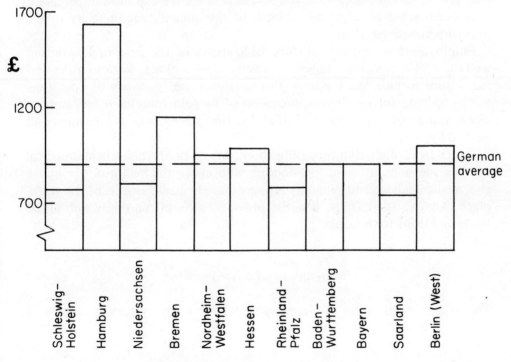

FIGURE 5.5   Average Incomes by Region

Table 2.9 the employer has to pay out a substantial element over and above the wages bill in fringe and social security benefits.

Sickness and disablement

Insurance against accidents and industrial diseases is compulsory. The system is administered through trade cooperative associations and other bodies, organised on an occupational or geographical basis. The employer contributes according to the risk of accident in his enterprise. Occupational diseases are indicated in an official list covering 47 illnesses.

Medical benefits comprise treatment and hospitalisation, on the same basis as in the sickness insurance scheme. In the case of temporary disability an insured person will receive his full wages and/or salary for the first six weeks and thereafter an allowance, as for sickness. A pension for permanent total disability amounts to 66.67 per cent of earnings, up to a maximum of DM 36,000 per annum. The pension is reduced according to the degree of disablement. In the event of death as a result of industrial accident or disease, the widow is entitled to a pension of 40 per cent of her late husband's earnings if she is over 45, is unable to work or has at least one dependent child, otherwise 30 per cent of earnings. Orphans receive 20 per cent for the loss of one parent, and 30 per cent for the loss of both parents.

A death grant equal to one-twelfth of the annual wage or salary of the insured person is payable.

Employers have many statutory obligations in the field of health and welfare, and are legally obliged to ensure safe working. Various rules and regulations include the pre-testing of machines and methods of operation, safety training for employees, provision of first-aid equipment etc, and lay down standards of lighting, ventilation, fire precautions, cloakrooms and general hygiene.

Apart from their statutory obligations, many employers provide medical services and appoint company doctors who check the health of personnel, give medical advice and generally advise on the hygienic aspects of the workplace. Among other fringe benefits provided are canteen meals, subsidised travel and loans for housing.

Retirement and other pensions

The biggest single item in Germany's social security system is retirement pensions, since the elderly constitute a large part of the population. (About 10.5 per cent of men and 21.9 per cent of women are of pensionable age.) The normal retiring age is 65, but a woman who has worked for 10 years in the past 20, can receive a pension at 60. Contributions amount to 17 per cent of assessed earnings (8.5 per cent each from employer and insured person) up to a ceiling of DM 25,200 (1972) per annum. There is also a government contribution.

The State pension accrues at the rate of 1.5 per cent of assessed earnings per year of credited service, with adjustments for national wages and various credits according to education, war service, university etc. For a full working career, it usually amounts to 40-45 per cent of final salary, or wages up to the ceiling.

The actual size of the pension depends on several elements, ie on the period during which a worker has contributed, his average wage or salary during the three years before retirement and the general development of wages, known as the dynamic pension. Since 1957 pensions have risen by about 120 per cent. Anybody who wishes to continue in work is able to do so. Pensions are also adjusted to take account of changes in the cost of living.

The pensions scheme is administered by insurance companies operating in the Länder; there are separate institutes for office workers, miners, seamen and railwaymen.

Despite the extensive coverage provided in the State system, there are many company-sponsored pensions schemes. It is estimated that about 80 per cent of companies employing over 100 workers have such arrangements, usually on a company basis. In addition there is a voluntary supplementary scheme called 'Höherversicherung' in which rates vary according to age.

Widows and orphans are entitled to pensions under the State and voluntary schemes. The amounts vary according to their husband's earnings or pension entitlement. If the widow is over 45, disabled or caring for a child, she should get 60 per cent of the State pension. Orphans get 10 per cent for the loss of one, and 20 per cent for the loss of two, parents.

Disability pensions accrue at the same rate as the State old age pension.

Family allowance

In Germany, as in the UK, no family allowance is paid for the first child. The monthly allowance for the second child is DM 25, for the third DM 50, for the fourth DM 60 and for the fifth and subsequent children DM 70. The normal age limit is 18. The Exchequer bears the cost of the scheme.

Unemployment benefit

Unemployment insurance is compulsory for all workers, whatever they earn. Contributions amount to 1.3 per cent of earnings up to a ceiling of DM 2,100 a month, shared equally between employer and employed. Benefits range from 40 to 60 per cent of earnings plus supplements for dependants.

LABOUR RELATIONS AND PROCEDURES

Labour matters are dealt with by the Federal Ministry of Labour and Social Affairs. The employment service is administered by a semi-autonomous Federal Labour Institute under the nominal supervision of the Ministry.

Recruitment and contract of employment

An employer is legally obliged to notify the local placement bureau within three days of hiring or firing a worker, including collective dismissals due to redundancies or disputes. Foreign workers are taken on under a special procedure — they need labour and residence permits. Employers are expected to offer jobs to a proportion of disabled workers and elderly people.

A typical contract of employment specifies such points as the duration of the contract, hours, overtime, accommodation and fare arrangements. It specifies the remuneration, whether fixed by contract, collective agreement, or custom. Contracts are terminated by mutual agreement or upon their expiry. Dismissal need not be in writing, nor need a reason be given, except in the case of salaried personnel. Salaried staff are normally entitled to six weeks notice. Manual workers can expect two weeks. Any disputes over a contract of employment have to be referred to the Court for Labour Affairs.

Collective bargaining

Labour relations in Germany operate within a legalistic framework. The basic legislation is covered by the Civil Code, supplemented by Codes for industry, crafts and agriculture. The Collective Agreements Act 1949, consolidated in 1969, makes collective agreements legally binding. Another Law in 1952 established minimum working conditions and an Act of 1963 governs minimum holidays.

Within this framework, employers and trade unions enjoy a wide degree of autonomy in collective bargaining. Although agreements have to be reported to the Federal Minister of Labour, and registered, this does not impede free negotiation. Collective bargaining is carried out at a number of levels. The most important negotiations are those at national or industry-wide level, which set out the basic guidelines for regional or local negotiations, and determine the 'master' agreement for the industry.

Most agreements cover wage rates, hours, holidays, periods of notice and social welfare arrangements. The usual period of their validity is two years, in some cases longer. As in the UK there is an increasing trend towards direct company negotiations, but the employers' associations are not anxious to encourage this.

Once made, a collective agreement becomes legally enforceable and strikes are forbidden during the currency of the agreement.

Most agreements include provisions for conciliation and mediation, based on a model conciliation agreement negotiated in 1954, eg in metal-working, building, printing, chemicals and maritime transport. Arbitration is purely voluntary, and both sides of industry are anxious to avoid compulsory Government arbitration. There is a system of Labour Courts, which have the responsibility of enforcing collective agreements. They operate at local and regional level, and the supreme authority is the Federal Labour Court. Most disputes are settled in local Courts. The German workers accept the intrusion of the law into industrial relations to a far greater extent than do the British.

Another legal requirement, contained in an Act of 1961, and revised in 1965 and 1970, concerns the accumulation of savings by the workers. Employers are given tax incentives to enable them to pay bonuses to their employees, which are earmarked for investment. These may take the form of the acquisition of shares in the company, or savings for house purchase and similar purposes.

In general, the climate of labour relations throughout West Germany is peaceful and favourable to the promotion of productivity. This is because of the high degree of cooperation between management and the trade unions. German unions do not believe in industrial action to settle disputes, except as a last resort, nor are they exclusively concerned with wages.

Between 1961 and 1970, the annual average number of days lost per 1,000 workers in industry was only 23, compared with 1,093 in Italy. Under guidelines laid down by the union leadership, an affiliated union can call a strike involving employment conditions (not a political strike) only if all negotiation procedures have been exhausted and if a secret ballot shows at least 75 per cent of the members eligible to vote to be in favour. Union statutes further stipulate that members then must follow the instructions of their executives. This effectively rules out the possibility of unofficial or wildcat strikes, although in 1969 there was a series of unofficial strikes in the metal industry; and there has been a growing militancy, especially among engineering workers.

Employers have the right to impose a lock-out, granted by the Federal Labour Court in 1955, but there have been no cases of their taking the first step.

Trade unions and employers

There are two national employers' organisations. The Federation of German Industry (BDI) deals with economic and commercial affairs. The Confederation of German Employers (BDA) is concerned with social policies. Formed in 1950, the BDA represents associations in almost every branch of private industry. Employers' associations and regional associations are affiliated. The Confederation does not itself engage in collective bargaining, but may draw up model agreements for the guidance of its affiliated associations. It advises the Government on aspects of employment policy. It operates through a General assembly, an Executive Board, a Presidential Board and an Executive Office, which is organised into departments covering such subjects as the law, wages policy, training and industrial relations. The BDA headquarters are in Cologne.

The trade union movement in West Germany is wealthy and influential. In 1933 there were well over 200 unions, but as a result of the postwar reconstruction (in which British assistance was given) the number of unions affiliated to the 'Deutscher Gewerkschaftbund' (equivalent to the TUC) was reduced to 16. These cover workers in building, mining, chemicals, printing, railways, education, agriculture, metals, commerce, plastics, artists, leather workers, foods, public services, postal services and textiles. There are 6.7 million members, and the biggest single union is the Metalworkers' Union, with over 2 million members.

About 400,000 salaried workers belong to the white collar union (DAG) and the civil servants have their own organisation (DBB).

The German economy has benefited enormously from the centralisation of union power and organisation on an industrial basis which effectively rule out demarcation disputes. The DGB has played an important part in stimulating productivity. It is highly professional, non-sectarian and non-political, though it is in sympathy with the SPD. The DGB headquarters are in

Düsseldorf, in an ultra-modern building which cost about DM 20 million in 1967. The unions have their own bank (fourth largest in the Republic) and run newspapers, insurance societies and housing schemes. There are 14 trade union schools and five DGB Federation schools as well as numerous local education and training courses.

Works councils

The Germans do not have a system of shop steward representation at plant level as there is in Britain. Shop steward functions are undertaken by works' councils, which are legally obligatory in every enterprise. These councils take up grievances, and deal with matters of safety, welfare and general issues affecting the workers (though not wages negotiations). Members are elected for three years by all workers in a factory, whether or not they are union members.

The employer is obliged to pay for election costs, release council members to attend meetings during working hours and provide them with the necessary facilities.

German unions attach great importance to the principle of 'Mitbestimmung' or co-determination, which is in the forefront of their programme. 'Mitbestimmung' was originally introduced in the iron and steel and coal industries in 1951, and provides for equal representation of shareholders and workers on the Supervisory Board (Aufsichtsrat) which controls policy. The workers also have the effective say in the appointment of the Labour Director to the Management Board (Vorstand). In 1952 the law was extended to private enterprise, providing for one-third worker representation on the 'Aufsichtsrat'.

Following intensive union pressure to extend the powers of Works' Councils, the Brandt Government introduced a new law in January 1972 to replace the 1952 law. This gives a works' council enhanced powers, though it does not go as far as the unions would have wished. A council can insist on co-determination in such matters as the period of the working day, the time and method of paying wages, holidays, social welfare provision, housing and methods of remuneration. It has the right to be consulted about personnel policy on recruitment, employment, transfers and dismissals.

An employer must seek the consent of the council before undertaking any re-deployment of labour. If there is disagreement over any issue, he must refer the matter to the Labour Court.

He can only dismiss an employee after he has notified the works' council,

83

which can raise objections within three days. The employee concerned has the right to apply to the Labour Court.

Managements must consult their councils before introducing any major changes in production methods. Council members now have full rights of access to the plant, instead of having to seek management permission. They enjoy reasonable protection against dismissal.

Not surprisingly, the West German employers, who accepted the original Law, expressed strong opposition to the inroads on managerial authority represented by the 1972 measures. A statement issued at the time by the BDA declared:

'The kind of co-determination demanded by the trade unions brings no advantages. Our free economic and social system, whose undeniable successes benefit us all, is based on a balance of forces. Extension of trade union co-determination would upset this balance and thus destroy the whole system.'

6

Italy

GENERAL

Italy covers a territory of 301,200 square kilometres and has a total population of 54,459,000 (1970). Its density of population is 181 per square kilometre. Apart from metropolitan Italy, the Vatican City, with about 1,000 inhabitants, covers 0.44 square kilometres, and the Republic of San Marino, with 20,000 inhabitants, an area of 61 square kilometres.

Italy has experienced a phenomenal economic growth since 1950 and is today one of the leading industrial countries of Europe. The gross national product was £34,250 million in 1969, of which industry accounted for 38.9 per cent and agriculture for 11.3 per cent. The index of industrial production rose during the past decade from 69 in 1959 (1963 = 100) to 139 in 1969 – the same growth rate as France. The most rapidly expanding industrial sectors include steel, chemicals and petro-chemicals, textiles and artificial fibres, motor vehicles, paper production and furniture. Agriculture still plays an important, if diminishing role, in the economy. The main crops are wheat, rice, olive oil, grapes, sugar beet and fruits, and there is a thriving export trade in fruit, vegetables and wine.

Italy has few natural resources. Sulphur is found in Sicily, iron ore in the island of Elba and Valle d'Aosta, and there are small deposits of zinc and lead, and a substantial amount of mercury. The marble industry, largely concentrated in Tuscany, is an important source of wealth.

Most raw materials have to be imported. Italy's main exports consist of machinery, especially precision tools, domestic appliances, vehicles, chemicals, textiles, clothing, and footwear. Tourism is a major source of revenue. About two-fifths of Italian exports are to EEC countries, from which it takes about a third of its imports, (a lower proportion than for any of the Six). A healty trade is maintained with EFTA countries and the USA.

The production of chemicals has trebled in the past ten years and the plastics industry has been a pace-setter. But perhaps the most spectacular development has been in the exploitation of oil and natural gas. More than 2,000 oil wells are active and refining capacity totals about 135 million tons a year, compared with 2.2 million tons before the War and 3 million tons in 1948. Oil meets 80 per cent of Italy's energy requirements. A thriving industry, based on petroleum products and derivatives has been developed and in 1971, over 20 million tons of petroleum products were sold in domestic and overseas markets. Production of natural gas rose from 2,000 million cubic metres in 1953 to 10,400 million cubic metres in 1969, and 13,000 million cubic metres in 1971. The Italians claim the longest pipeline in Europe for distributing natural gas.

Italy has been a democratic Republic since 1946 and adopted its Constitution in 1948. The President, whose term of office is seven years, is Head of State and nominates the Council of Ministers, led by the Prime Minister. Parliament is bi-cameral, with a Chamber of Deputies consisting of 630 members elected by direct universal suffrage and a Senate, with 315 members elected on a regional basis. The political scene is unstable. There have been 34 different administrations since the end of the War, and five Governments since 1968. A centre-left coalition of Christian Democrats, Socialists and Republicans was formed in August 1970, but the elections of 1972 resulted in the formation of a predominantly Christian-Liberal coalition, with a narrow majority under Signor Andreotti. The main political groups in the Chamber are the Christian Democrats (DC), Communists (PCI), Socialists and Social Democrats (PSI), Social Movement (MSI) and Liberals (PLI). The Christian Democrats have been the leading party since the end of the War.

Successive Italian Governments have done much to stimulate economic growth. A number of State organisations have been set up to supervise and control various industries. These include the Institute for Industrial Reconstruction (IRI) which controls and supervises steel, shipbuilding, mechanical engineering, telephones, radio/TV, maritime and air transport and highways, and ENI, the national hydrocarbons authority. The State generally avoids

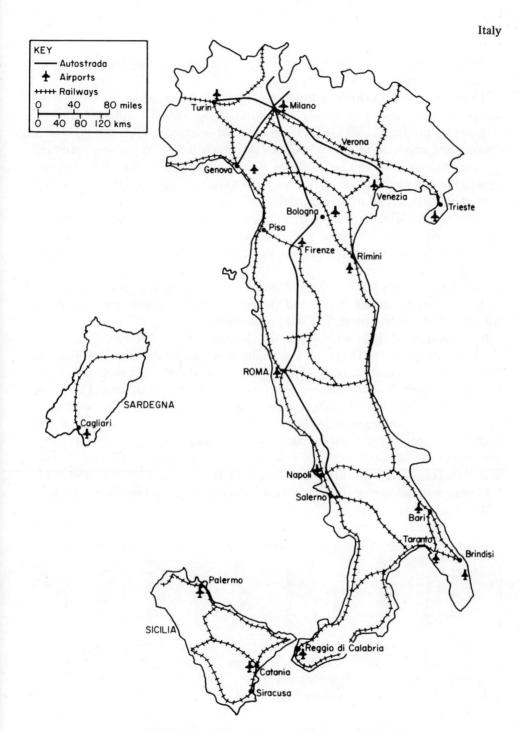

KEY
— Autostrada
✈ Airports
┼┼┼┼ Railways
0   40   80 miles
0   40   80   120 kms

Turin

Milano

Verona

Genova

Venezia

Trieste

Bologna

Pisa

Firenze

Rimini

SARDEGNA

Cagliari

ROMA

Napoli

Salerno

Bari

Taranto

Brindisi

Palermo

SICILIA

Reggio di Calabria

Catania

Siracusa

FIGURE 6.1   Major Centres and Communications

direct economic action, leaving the State holding companies to act as commercial enterprises.

Thus, ENI operates through three corporations: AGIP, which is responsible for prospecting and production of hydrocarbons and the distribution of petroleum products; SNAM, responsible for methane and oil pipelines, tankers and scientific research, and ANIC, which is responsible for refining, petro-chemicals and textiles. A State Board is responsible for all electricity generation and distribution throughout the country. Another State Authority promotes the interests of artisan trades.

Through the Ministry of the Budget and Economic Planning, the Government prepares a series of economic plans, which lay down the main guidelines for expansion, set out priorities for investment and identify particular targets to be achieved.

Administratively, Italy is divided into 20 regions, eight in the North, four in the Centre, six in the South and two in the Islands (Sicily and Sardinia). Nearly half the total population lives in the North.

The majority of Italians belong to the Roman Catholic Church.

Despite the massive range of mountains which separate Italy from France, Switzerland and Austria, road and rail communications are excellent, owing to the engineering achievements in tunnelling and road-building. There are altogether 17,000 km of railway lines and a large road network, of which 3,500 km are modern motorways — Italy comes second to Germany in its mileage of motorways. Civil aviation has developed since the War, and there are airports at Rome (1 hour by road from the city), Milan, Genoa, Venice and Palermo, with new airports being constructed at Florence and Bari. Frequent services are operated by BEA, Alitalia and all international airlines to the main centres of Italy.

'000s	Agriculture	Manufacturing	Building	Other Industrial	Commerce	Transport	Other Services	TOTAL
1968	4,247	5,675	1,922	293	2,630	985	3,317	19,069
1971	3,652	5,977	1,977	291	2,508	1,001	3,847	18,893

Source: Ministry of Labour and Social Security

TABLE 6.2   Analysis of Employment by Sector

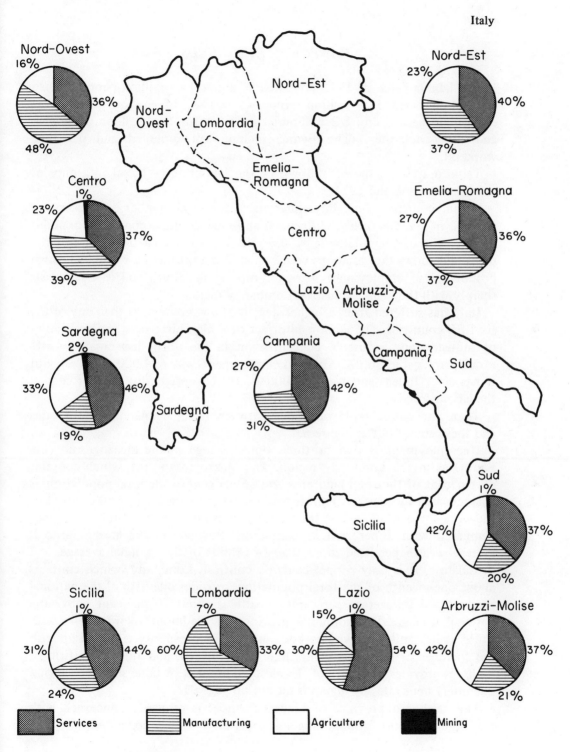

Italy

FIGURE 6.3 Employment Profiles by Region

MANPOWER RESOURCES

Italy's labour force in 1971 consisted of about 19.5 million people (14.25 million men and 5.25 million women). Of this, 3.6 million people were engaged in agriculture, 8.2 million in industry and 7.04 million in services and other activities. (The figures include self-employed and part-time workers).

Table 6.2 shows the breakdown of the labour force by main groups of activities in 1968 and 1971.

Within industry, some three-quarters of the total number of workers are engaged in manufacturing, with metal and engineering accounting for about 25 per cent of the total. Figure 6.3 gives a further breakdown of employment and shows the variations which exist in the profiles by region. The high proportion of employment in agriculture in the south and east contrasts sharply with the highly industrial Lombardia region.

Italy has suffered from a higher degree of unemployment than any of the six EEC countries. The combined effect of a high birth rate, rationalisation of industry and industrial concentration in the north has created acute problems for the south. Total unemployment was 694,000 in 1968, but it has since fallen, and was 613,000 in 1971, representing 3.1 per cent of the labour force.

There are considerable variations between regional unemployment rates and these are set out in Figure 6.4.

Unemployment is two or three times as high in the Mezzogiorno (the South) as in the Lombardy region. The Mezzogiorno area, which contains 40 per cent of the total land area and 36 per cent of the total population, is characterised by poverty, remoteness and backwardness. Over 40 per cent of the work-force is engaged on the land, which is infertile and barely cultivable, compared with 7 per cent in Lombardy. Nowhere in the Mezzogiorno is average wealth per head more than two-thirds of the national average, and in Calabria, it is only 49 per cent. By contrast, Lombardy, which contains about one-seventh of the total population, provides one-fifth of the national product and its average per capita wealth is about 50 per cent above the national average. The adjoining province of Piedmont (Nord-Ouest) with Turin as its capital, is likewise booming and its prosperity is bound up with the fortunes of industrial giants like Fiat, Olivetti, and the textile firm of Biella. It provides one-tenth of the national product. A table showing varying unemployment rates by region is set out on page 91.

The sea-board province of Liguria (Genoa) is primarily concerned with maritime transport, shipbuilding and tourism. This over-congested industrial

(1968 %)	
Nord-Ouest	2.2
Lombardia	1.9
Nord-Est	2.4
Emilia-Romagna	2.7
Centro	2.9
Lazio	4.2
Compania	4.3
Abruzzi-Molise	4.6
Sud	5.1
Sicilia	3.7
Sardegna	4.8
Italy — National Average	3.2

Source: EEC

TABLE 6.4   Regional Unemployment Rates

triangle, Lombardy-Piedmont-Liguria, is at the hub of Italy's economy.

Because of the lack of employment opportunities, there has been a mass migration of people from the south. Since the end of the War, about six million people left the south, over two million during the 1960s. In addition to moving to north Italy, many southern Italians have found work in EEC countries and Switzerland.

Successive Italian Governments have long been concerned with the need to help the under-developed areas of the south. In 1950 a Development Fund for Southern Italy was set up, to provide regional assistance through a system of incentives. These include capital grants of 20 per cent for investment in industrial buildings and 30 per cent for plant and machinery; loans at low rates of interest; a 10-year exemption from corporation tax and a 50 per cent reduction in turnover tax, excise duty on motor vehicles and certain railway freight rates. The Government in addition allocates at least 40 per cent of public sector investment to the south. From 1971 to 1976, it will spend up to 7,200,000 million lire or more than the total in the past 22 years. A law of October 1971 laid down that southern development should be treated as the central priority in national planning, and obliged State and private enterprises to locate massive investment projects in the region.

Many firms have already taken advantage of the concessions and have found additional attractions, in the availability of labour, lower costs, and fewer restrictions than in the industrial north.

The main focal-point of new development is a triangle in Apulia, based on Bari, Taranto and Brindisi, but Sicily, Catania and Calabria are all acquiring a share of new industry.

At the outset, the Development Fund was devoted mainly towards building up the infra-structure, with projects not only for physical improvements such as roads, ports, land reclamation, irrigation, housing and drainage, but providing loans for hotels, schools, health services and training centres. The current emphasis is on attracting large-scale industry, steel, engineering and chemicals, with an accompanying leaven of small-scale firms and service trades, which have more effect on local employment than the capital-intensive industries.

Considerable success has been claimed for the Italian regional policies. The numbers employed in the southern provinces have increased and there is less migration to the north.

One problem met by industrialists is that of adapting to factory conditions the peasants and workers who come straight from the farms and vineyards, and in a hot climate are used to a very different tempo of life from the northerners. The Italian Ministry of Labour is responsible for training, and increasing emphasis is being placed on vocational training for adults in the current economic Plan.

Other regions, eg the agricultural areas of the Centre and the extreme North and Veneto, have serious employment problems, but they are not on the same scale as those of the Mezzogiorno.

Since April 1972, greater autonomy is being given to each region to promote its own economic development. (See *The Times* 21 June 1972.)

WAGES

Wages in the Italian Republic have risen steeply during the past two decades, but as the original base was lower than in other EEC countries, the Italian worker's income is below the level of the other countries of the Common Market. Between April 1964 and October 1971 there was a 75 per cent rise in the earnings of male manual workers and one of 87 per cent in those of women.

The cost of living has risen, but not as steeply as in France and the Netherlands. The consumer price index (1963 = 100) was 134.4 in 1971.

The ten highest paid industrial groups (October 1970) were coalmining, natural gas, petroleum products, non-metallic mining, printing and publishing, aircraft, automobiles, tobacco, iron and steel, and transport (in that order).

Disparities between industrial workers' earnings are very wide. A recent analysis by the International Labour Office gives the following breakdown of average hourly rates for selected occupations.

Hourly rates in Milan at October 1971	
	Lira
Clothing, men's shirts	503
Furniture	612
Printing and Publishing	615 - 954
Chemicals	561
Engineering (skilled)	474 - 522
(labourers)	408
Garage mechanics	525
Building (tradesmen)	775
(labourers	663
Electricians (skilled)	892
(unskilled)	620
Railways, unskilled	457
Bus, tram drivers	545 - 595
Lorry drivers	542

Source: ILO

TABLE 6.5   Wage Rates in Selected Industries

Rates in Milan are slightly higher than those in Rome, Genoa and Naples. Figure 6.6 charts the varying levels of incomes between regions which existed in 1968.

Examples of monthly rates for salaried employees are retail sales assistants (124,080 Lire) and laboratory assistants (208,221 Lire).

Despite the Treaty of Rome provisions on equal pay, there is still a gap between earnings for men and women, but Italy has gone farther than any other EEC country in closing it by escalating the female rate of increase. In the manufacture of metal goods, electrical and non-electrical machinery, the

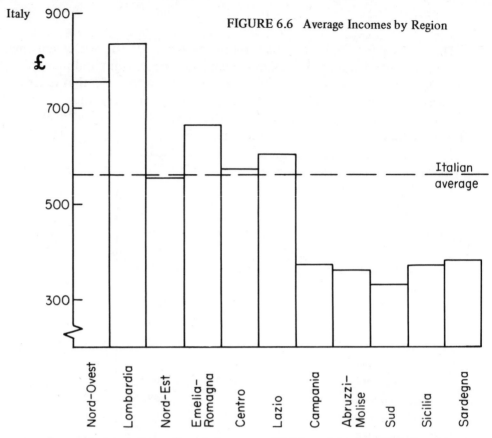

Italy

FIGURE 6.6 Average Incomes by Region

£

Italian average

Nord–Ovest
Lombardia
Nord–Est
Emelia–Romagna
Centro
Lazio
Campania
Abruzzi–Molise
Sud
Sicilia
Sardegna

women's percentage of men's earnings was 83-86 and in the vehicles group, it was 88 (October 1970).

The length of the working week is determined by collective agreement, and the standard in 1972 was 40-42, depending on the branch of industry. There are variations even within the same industry; thus motor vehicle and aircraft workers have a 40-hour agreement, whereas shipbuilding workers work 42 hours, though this was to be reduced to 40 at the end of 1972. The actual number of hours worked (April 1971) was 42.2 throughout industry. Overtime is paid on basic hourly rates, including the cost of living bonus, at 20 per cent for the first two hours and 30 per cent beyond.

The Italians enjoy longer holidays than any other EEC workers. The minimum laid down by collective agreement is 13-21 days, and there are 17 public holidays, making a total of 30-38 days, This includes arrangements for extra days, according to age and length of service (two days after three years, four after ten and five after 19 years). Holiday pay is calculated on full pay plus five per cent for daily-paid workers and average earnings for piece-workers.

Under laws of 1949, 1954 and 1958, there are 17 public holidays —
January 1st, Epiphany, (January 6), St Joseph's Day (19 March), Anniversary
of the Liberation (25 April) Easter Monday, Ascension Day, Corpus Christi,
May Day, National Liberation Day (2 June), St Peter and St Paul (29 June),
Assumption of the Virgin Mary (15 August), All Saints Day (1 November),
National Unity Day (4 November), Immaculate Conception Day (8 December),
Christmas Day and Boxing Day (25 and 26 December).

All Government offices, local government offices, schools and banks are
closed.

There are half-day holidays on 11 February, 28 September, 4 October, the
last day of Carnival, the Thursday before Easter, 2 November, 24 December
and 31 December.

SOCIAL SECURITY

Even if he is less well paid than his opposite numbers in Europe, the Italian
worker receives compensation in generous provision for fringe benefits and

July 1970 – Percentage of Earnings				
	Total	Employer	Worker	State
Sickness and maternity[1]	14.60	14.46 [2]	0.15	State subsidises any deficit
Invalidity and old age pension	20.80	13.90	6.90	Financing of social fund
Family allowances	-	17.50	-	Annual subsidies
Unemployment	-	2.30	-	State contribution + unemployment assistance

[1] Includes 3.80 per cent for pensioners' sickness insurance, 2 per cent for tuberculosis and
0.58 per cent for agricultural solidarity.

[2] Rates for non-industrial staff are: 12.61, Industry; 12.89, Commerce and 11.28 per cent
Banks and Insurance.

Source: EEC – Comparative tables of the Social Security System of the
European Communities.

TABLE 6.7 Contributions to Social Security Costs

social security payments. It is estimated that the cost of these benefits (including holidays and bonuses) amounts to 85 to 90 per cent of basic pay. In fact, the cost of these benefits nearly doubles the cost of employing one man.

The scheme places a heavy burden on employers, who bear the brunt of financing it. The financial contributions by the two sides of industry can be conveniently set out (see Table 6.7).

Benefits, as well as contributions, are related to earnings, The social security scheme covers sickness and maternity, old age, disability, and survivors' pensions, industrial injuries and occupational diseases, family allowances and unemployment. It comes under the general supervision of the Ministry of Labour and Social Insurance and is administered through offices of three separate Institutions – the National Institute for Social Security (INPS) which is responsible for all schemes apart from sickness, and industrial injuries. The former is dealt with by a National Sickness Institute (INAM) and the latter by a National Accident Insurance Institute (INAIL).

Sickness and disablement

Sickness and disablement benefits are available to insured people and their dependants. They include medical and dental treatment, hospitalisation and medicines up to a maximum of 180 days in one year (with possible extension). Cash allowances start on the fourth day of sickness at 50 per cent of daily earnings and after 21 days are raised to 66.6 per cent. There is a maximum period of 180 days a year. Non-industrial staff do not receive cash benefits, but the employer must by law pay their salaries for at least three months.

Industrial injuries and diseases are the responsibility of the employer, who contributes according to the risk, averaging about 3.90 per cent of earnings. Cash benefits start on the fourth day and continue until recovery; they amount to 60 per cent of average daily earnings over the past fortnight, and after 90 days are increased to 75 per cent. In practice the employer pays 100 per cent of the earnings on the day of the accident, and 60 per cent in the three following days.

Medical benefits include medical, general and specialist treatment, hospitalisation and surgical applicances, and continue until recovery.

In the case of permanent disablement, pensions are assessed according to the degree of disablement. There is a constant attendance allowance of Lire 35,000 a month and supplements for dependants. In the event of death, a widow is entitled to a pension amounting to 50 per cent of her late husband's annuity, and an orphan to 20 per cent. A lump sum is payable on death, varying from Lire 140,000 to 260,000, plus allowances for dependents. Rates are automatically adjusted according to the changes in the level of industrial earnings over the past three years.

Retirement and other pensions

All employed persons are covered in the general scheme, administered by INPS, which provides for retirement at 60 for men and 55 for women. There are special schemes for seamen, teachers, public servants and industrial managers. The pension is based on the average earnings of the best three periods of 52 consecutive weeks out of the last 260 weeks of contributions. The full pension accrued after 40 years amounts to 74 per cent of earnings, or 1.85 per cent per year of service, rising up to 80 per cent by 1976. The minimum is Lire 299,000 p.a. or Lire 325,000 for people over 65. There are supplements for married pensioners and for children under 18, equal to family allowances.

The pension is payable 13 times a year and is automatically adjusted according to the cost of living index.

Cumulation of the pension with income from employment is allowed for an amount equal to the minimum pension; if a pensioner is entitled to a higher pension, he can draw 50 per cent of the excess on the minimum up to Lire 100,000 a month.

Widows and orphans receive pensions, subject to a minimum of five years' contribution. The widow's pension is equal to 60 per cent of the insured person's actual or accrued old age pension. It ceases on re-marriage, when a lump sum equal to two years' pension is paid. Orphans under 18 are entitled to pensions equal to 20 per cent of the pension for the loss of one parent, and 40 per cent if both parents are dead.

There is a death grant of Lire 20,000.

Disability pensions are calculated on the same basis as old age pensions, with similar supplements for dependants. A worker is considered disabled if his earning capacity is reduced to one-third of normal earnings, one half in the case of clerical workers.

Managerial staffs are insured in a special Fund (INDPAI) and do not participate in the INPS scheme. Normal retiring age is 65 for men and 60 for women. Pensions vary according to contributions and after a full career of 30 years would amount to 80 per cent of average salary up to a ceiling, which is periodically adjusted. (1971 = Lire 13,903,500 per annum.) The scheme provides for survivors'and disability pensions.

Employers have to pay compulsory leaving service or seniority indemnities to their staffs, at the rate of at least one month's salary for each year of service, with more for senior executives. Such payments are not compulsory for manual workers, but employers customarily make a terminal payment, according to the length of service.

There would appear to be few arrangements for private pension plans.

Family and maternity allowances

Maternity benefits form part of the sickness insurance scheme. Insured women, the wife, daughters and sisters of insured persons are covered. Benefits comprise medical treatment at home or in hospital and a system of cash allowance.

These are paid for a period of three months before confinement and eight weeks after confinement for women working in industry, and for 14 weeks. six before confinement, for those in commerce, at the rate of 80 per cent of earnings.

Family allowances, paid for by the employer only, apply to all children up to the age of 18. The amounts are at a flat rate of Lire 5,720 per month per child. Unemployed people are entitled to allowances, and there are also benefits for dependents (wife or invalid husband, father or mother) subject to a means test. Allowances are higher for certain sectors, eg banks and insurance, and the highest rate is given to professional journalists.

Unemployment benefits

Unemployment benefits, paid for by the employer, are paid at a standard rate of Lire 400 a day, after a waiting period of seven days. Benefits last for a maximum period of 180 days. There is a provision for a daily supplement of Lire 120 for each dependent child under 16, (under 18 in the case of office workers) as well as for dependent parents who are entitled to family allowances.

LABOUR RELATIONS AND PROCEDURES

Labour matters are the responsibility of the Ministry of Labour and Social

Security. As well as dealing with all labour functions, eg employment, training, vocational guidance, manpower, industrial relations, inspection, safety, health and welfare, the Ministry supervises the administration of social insurance schemes through the institutes mentioned in the previous section. The Ministry operates through a network of 20 regional offices and 82 provincial offices.

Recruitment and contract of employment

All applications for engaging workers must be made through official employment exchanges. Employers have to notify these offices of engagements and dismissals and supply regular information about the numbers of workers and any changes in their work force. When hiring or firing an employee, the employer must notify the office within five days. The contract of employment is regarded as of unlimited duration, except in the case of a worker hired for a specific or seasonal job. Dismissals must be made in writing and reasons given. Length of notice varies in different industries and according to the employee's length of service. There is compensation for dismissal, according to length of service, and there are arrangements for redundancy pay if a worker loses his job through re-organisation or closure. These arrangements have the force of law.

Collective bargaining

In looking at the system of labour relations and collective bargaining in Italy, it is necessary to appreciate the background of 20 years of Fascism and five years of war during which free employers and unions were not allowed to exist. At the end of the war, there were few people on either side of industry with experience or expertise in voluntary and democratic procedures, and there was a tendency to impose a system of national top-level negotiation, almost on Corporate State lines. This in itself was partly responsible for the dissatisfaction of the workers and led to a sense of remoteness from the activities at the top.

In the last decade, a new pattern has emerged with a shift of emphasis from national to local plant levels. The tidal wave of labour unrest in 1969, which involved about four million workers, led to direct union talks with the Government and a virtual recognition of union rights at factory level. A so-called Workers' Charter was drawn up and in May 1970 was given the force of law, guaranteeing workers the right to engage in union activities at their place of work.

By 1970-71, a total of 4,400 plant agreements involving more than 1.5 million workers had been reached. The main purpose of plant bargaining is to prepare the ground for national agreements and secure additional gains at the local level.

The main basis of collective bargaining, however, remains the national collective contracts, negotiated between the unions and employers' organisations for most industries and commerce. They only apply to the signatory organisations but are accepted in law as laying down standards for the whole industry. Employment Exchange officials have to be satisfied that the wages and conditions offered to a worker are in line with those stipulated in the collective contract. Contracts are usually industry-based and cover both salaried staff and manual workers. They lay down general rules for employment, minimum rates of pay, hours, holidays etc.

Workers with grievances usually take these up through their delegates, who have shop steward functions, or their factory committees. Conciliation is provided through the Ministry of Labour mediation services, which act locally or centrally and can be called upon by either party. There is provision for voluntary arbitration and the Minister is empowered to intervene if a dispute threatens the public interest.

Labour relations in Italy are still unsettled, with the metal-workers in the automobile and engineering industries setting the pace. More working days have been lost through strikes than in any of the Ten countries, and the average between 1961 and 1970 was 1,093 per 1,000 persons, a figure only exceeded by Canada and the USA. The majority of strikes are of short duration; many are of a political character, or are called to press for social reforms.

Trade unions and employers

The majority of employers are organised in associations attached to Confindustria, the General Confederation of Italian Industry. This body has 105 area associations and 98 national industrial associations. The former are organised within the administrative provinces, and the latter normally cater for firms on an industrial basis. There is a separate organisation, Intersind, which organises management in industries where there is State participation (apart from oil and the public services), and which bargains separately.

The trade unions are divided on political lines. The strongest organisation is the General Confederation of Labour (CGIL) which is Communist-oriented and belongs to the World Federation of Trade Unions. It claims about 2½ million members and has set the pace in aggressive militancy. The Italian Confederation of Labour Unions (CISL) is largely dominated by Catholics, but contains a proportion of Republicans and anti-Communist socialists. It was formed in 1949 as a counter-balance to the CGIL, and now claims about 2 million members. The smaller Italian Union of Labour (UIL) is non-sectarian and independent of both Catholics and Communists, and has about half a million members. A small (76,000 members) neo-fascist and monarchist group is the National Workers Union Confederation (CISNAL). There is also a Radical Christian Association (ACLI) with about 600,000 members.

All these membership figures are probably exaggerated and it is unlikely that total union membership in Italy is as high as the figure of 50 per cent which is claimed for it. Even at the Fiat works in Turin, only one-third of the workers are organised. The company, in the paternalistic tradition which is common to Italian employers, operates many welfare schemes for the benefit of its workers, such as a private health service, housing, a hospital and a holiday resort in the Alps.

During the 1950s and early 1960s there was constant and often bitter warfare between the main groups, which weakened the whole movement. The CGIL, like the French GGT, tended to act politically in furtherance of the interests of the Italian Communist Party, while the CISL maintained very close links with the ruling Christian Democrat Party.

In recent years, however, there has been an abatement of Inter-union strife and the organisations have sought to co-ordinate their activities. Discussions on re-unification have been held, and agreement reached on a programme for unification by February 1973. There are however powerful political obstacles in the way of its achievement.

Most Italian unions are under-staffed and lack financial resources. This is one reason why they prefer lightning strikes and token stoppages, rather than prolonged confrontations. There is very little discipline exercised over rank and file membership from union headquarters.

Some unions are organised on industrial lines, eg engineering and ship-building, but most are on a territorial basis, and form a 'Chamber of Labour' in the locality. At plant level there are shop committees and workers' delegates (the equivalent of shop stewards). These committees are most active in engineering, where the metalworkers claim there are 22,000 delegates in 1,400 committees, textiles, clothing and rubber.

Works councils

The system of works councils is not compulsory but is dependent on voluntary agreement in enterprises employing more than 40 workers. Members are elected from lists prepared by non-union as well as union members. Their functions are advisory and mainly concerned with social and welfare matters, but they have the right to be informed about changes in manning, redundancy and hours and to make proposals on production policies and problems.

7

Luxembourg

GENERAL

The Grand Duchy of Luxembourg covers an area of about 2,600 square km and borders on France, Belgium and Germany. It has a population of about 340,000 and a population density of 131 per square km.

Despite its small size, Luxembourg is a prosperous country and indeed has the highest national income per head of any EEC country. In 1971 its GNP was 50,900 million Lux. francs; industry accounted for just over half and agriculture for about five per cent. The economy is largely dependent on steel which accounts for about 25 per cent of the GNP.

In recent years, to offset the dominance of the steel industry, the Government has sought to introduce new industries, including chemicals, the manufacture of tyres and commercial vehicles, tobacco and drink. There is little in the way of production of consumer goods. Agriculture and wine-growing still remain important sectors, though declining. More than half the country consists of agricultural land, and cattle-raising accounts for four-fifths of agricultural revenues.

The economic growth rate during the early 1960s was 3.5 per cent and it is estimated that it will continue between 3.5 and 4 per cent from 1970 to 1975.

The Grand Duchy possesses no natural resources, apart from iron ore, and has to rely on imports to keep industry going. Its trade is almost entirely intra-Community, with 90 per cent of its imports originating from EEC countries which take 75 per cent of its exports, Germany and Belgium being the main trading partners. Steel represents two-thirds of total exports, the balance being made up of plastic fibres, rubber and chemical products and textiles. Exports of iron ore, which at one time were over 1 million tons, have ceased and there are only nine mines in operation compared with 66 pre-war. Ore production fell from 7.8 m tons in 1957 to 4.5 m tons in 1971. Luxembourg obtains most of its ore supplies from France and its coke from Germany.

Tourism provides a healthy source of revenue. The most significant development in recent years has been the expansion of the banking sector and the rise of Luxembourg as an international financial centre. Between 1955 and 1971, the number of banking establishments rose from 13 to 43, with 449 agencies. There are 39 private insurance companies.

Luxembourg's industry is dominated by the steel industry giants, but for the most part, firms are small or medium-sized. A number of American subsidiaries, including Goodyear, Monsanto and Du Pont, operate in the modern industrial sector. As a result of an intensive dam-building programme on three main rivers, hydro-electricity is now supplying nearly half the country's energy needs, compared with only 1.4 per cent in 1960.

The Grand Duchy is an independent sovereign State, the Head of State being a hereditary prince. Executive power is vested in the Cabinet, led by the Prime Minister. There are two Houses — the Chamber of Deputies, with 56 members elected for a 5-year term by universal adult suffrage, and the Council of State, consisting of 21 members, which scrutinises bills submitted by the Chamber.

Luxembourg is an original member of the EEC and provided its original headquarters. It now houses the European Coal and Steel Community and various sections of the EEC, including the European Investment Bank. French and German are the official languages, though local people speak Luxembourgeois.

Because of the smallness of the country, there are few internal communications problems. Luxembourg has about 3,125 miles of road, and 170 miles of railway; both road and rail carry transit traffic from Belgium and the Netherlands to France, and Germany. There is an international airport, and a national airline LUXAIR, with flights to Brussels, London and the main European capitals. Passengers from the United Kingdom usually fly via Brussels.

MANPOWER RESOURCES

Of the total population in 1969, about 150,000 were actively employed. A breakdown of the employment position shows the following profile.

Per Cent	
Agriculture, forestry, etc	10
Mining and quarrying	2
Manufacturing	44
Construction	7
Commerce and Services	37

Source: Official Government Statistics

TABLE 7.1 Analysis of Employment by Sector

There is no unemployment in Luxembourg and the country relies heavily on immigrant labour. In January 1971, 80,000 people, or about 25 per cent of the population, were classified as foreigners. The great majority came from other EEC countries — Italians, 33,000; Germans, 11,500; French, 9,000; Belgians, 6,000; Dutch, 2,000; non-EEC groups included Portuguese, 9,000; Spanish, 4,500; and Americans 1,500.

Over half the foreigners live in the Luxembourg city area, a quarter in the Esch-sur-Aezette area and the balance in the Diekirch locality. Most work in building, where over 80 per cent of the workers are foreign, manufacturing, general and domestic service trades and in jobs which, given a state of full employment, do not attract the native Luxembourgeois.

The Government has pursued a policy of encouraging integration and has managed to ease housing and education problems for immigrants.

Hostels have been provided for single workers, particularly from Spain and Italy, and special language courses arranged for school children and adults. The programmes are coordinated through an 'Immigrants' Social Service' organisation.

Regional problems as such do not exist within the Grand Duchy. The main concern is to achieve a greater degree of diversification. The steel giant ARBED-HADIR, producing steel, iron ore, metal and non-ferrous metal products, employs 24,000 workers (1971) and a smaller steel company employs 2,900. Enterprises employing between 1,000 and 5,000 workers include the railways, Goodyear and Monsanto.

WAGES

Luxembourg comes second to West Germany in the 'League Table' of earnings in manufacturing. The top ten industries in October 1970 were metallic ore mining, preparation of metallic ores, iron and steel, metal manufacturing, printing and publishing, synthetic fibres, rubber and plastics, foundries, non-ferrous metals manufacturing and non-metallic mining (in that order).

The lower-paid groups included textiles, clothing and footwear, and furniture.

The general rate of wage increase was slower than in other EEC countries. Taking 1964 as 100, the index of average hourly gross earnings increased to 160 by 1971 and the consumer price index rose to 125, which was a smaller rise than for any EEC country.

Wages are linked to the retail price index. They must be paid in cash, at least once a month.

Equal pay is applied in principle, but in practice there is not much scope for women to work in a country so dominated by heavy industry. The rate of women's earnings has risen more steeply than that of the men.

The standard working week, fixed by law, provides for a 44½ hour week, normally on a five-day week basis. The average hours manual workers actually worked in October 1970 were 44 in manufacturing and 45 in all industries, more than 50 hours a week being worked in some sections of steel and engineering. In December 1970 an Act was passed providing for a two-stage reduction in hours, reaching the 40 hour week in January 1975. Overtime is paid at 30 per cent of the basic hourly rate for the first four hours, but in practice little overtime is worked.

Permission to work longer than the legal maximum must be obtained from the Labour Inspectorate.

Holiday entitlement is 16½ days annual paid leave, with additional days according to service and age, and 10 public holidays. Payments are based on average hourly earnings. Employees under 18 receive an additional 6½ days because of their youth.

SOCIAL SECURITY

The social security system is fully comprehensive, covering health, workmen's compensation, old age and invalidity and children's allowances, non-contributory unemployment benefits and public assistance. Most of the services are run by semi-public bodies, which include representatives of employers and employees, under the general supervision of the appropriate Government department.

Sickness and disablement

All workers are covered and there are separate schemes for public employees, miners, railwaymen etc. The employer pays two per cent and a manual worker four per cent on earnings up to Lf 219,000 a year. (The State pays 50 per cent of the administrative cost). Benefits include medical expenses and cash allowances, ranging from 50 to 70 per cent of the basic wage for 26 weeks.

For salaried workers, benefits are limited to a partial refund (between 80 and 100 per cent) of medical expenses. Employers are obliged to pay their staffs at full salary during illness.

Disability pensions are calculated on the same basis as the old age pension, provided the insured person is at least two-thirds disabled.

Benefits for industrial injuries and occupational diseases are paid for exclusively by the employer. They comprise the refunding of the cost of medical treatment and compensation for loss of wages, amounting to 75 per cent of daily earnings for 13 weeks, and thereafter amounts varying according to incapacity with a maximum of 80 per cent of daily earnings in the case of total incapacity (plus a constant attendance allowance).

Benefits for widows and orphans vary according to earnings.

The scheme is administered by a special Assurance Association.

Retirement and other pensions

There are separate arrangements for wage earners and salaried employees, the main differences being the imposition of an earnings ceiling Lf 367.200 for salaried employees and varying conditions for early retirement. In both cases employer and employee pay seven per cent. The State pays the full basic part of the pension, plus 50 per cent of administrative costs.

The basic pension is 15,000 francs per annum adjusted annually in line with the cost of living index, bringing it in 1972 to 27,000 francs. In addition there is a 1.6 per cent increment of average salary or wages for each year of service. The maximum pension may not exceed $83\frac{1}{3}$ per cent of average earnings during the employee's most favourable years of insurance. The minimum guaranteed pension is 39,120 francs. Subject to qualifying conditions, the widow of a salaried employee is entitled to a pension of two-thirds of the basic amount and 60 per cent of the annual increment. The widow of a wage earner receives the same basic amount but only 50 per cent of the increment. Orphans' pensions amount to one-third of the basic and 20 per cent of the increment.

Normal retirement age is 65, but earlier retirement at 62 for wage-earners and 60 for salaried workers (55 for women) is optional provided the necessary qualifying conditions have been met. There is a death grant, amounting to one-fifteenth of annual earnings.

The generous scale of State pensions leaves little scope for private arrangements, except for higher-paid executives, who come above the social security ceiling.

Family and maternity allowances

Family allowances are paid for exclusively by the employer, amount to Lf 619 a month for the first and second children, and Lf 1,117 for the third and subsequent children. The normal age limit is 19. There are also arrangements for birth allowances.

Insured women receive hospitalisation and an allowance of 50 to 75 per cent of insurable earnings for 12 weeks as a maternity benefit. Birth grants of Lf 7,035 are paid for each birth.

Unemployment benefit

Unemployment insurance covers employed persons under 65. There are two waiting days and benefits last for 26 weeks. Benefit amounts to 60 per cent of insurable earnings up to Lf 600 per day. It can be drawn by workers who are only partly unemployed.

LABOUR RELATIONS AND PROCEDURES

The National Labour Office, under the auspices of the Ministry of Labour, is responsible for manpower matters, employment services, vocational guidance, recruitment of foreign workers and the administration of unemployment insurance.

Recruitment and contract of employment

The Office has a monopoly of placements (except for managerial personnel), and every employer must notify its local office of vacancies, specifying the nature of the job and the conditions of employment. Employers of more than 50 workers are obliged to employ a proportion of disabled and handicapped workers.

Employment contracts are usually made in writing and may include provision for a trial period. They can be cancelled by mutual agreement and the employer is obliged to give the reasons for ending the contract, if requested to do so by the worker.

Collective bargaining

Collective bargaining determines wages and working conditions throughout the Grand Duchy, but minimum wage rates are fixed by law. Once a collective agreement has been decided on by the representative joint labour-management committee and signed, the Government normally extends its application to all the workers in the industry concerned. The contract remains in force unless it is denounced three months before it is due to expire. Wages are linked to the retail price index.

Strikes and lock-outs are illegal until the prescribed procedure for concluding collective contracts has been followed. Most contracts lay down procedures for dealing with industrial disputes and for reference to conciliation and arbitration. The Government runs a conciliation service, which can intervene without waiting for an invitation, but does not impose its decisions. Arbitration is not compulsory, but both parties may agree to voluntary arbitration. Labour Courts deal with disputed interpretations of employment contracts.

Trade unions and employers

The climate of labour-management relations is conducive to industrial peace. The employers' main organisation is the Federation of Luxembourg Industrialists. There are two separate trade union centres — the Confédération Générale du Travail (CGT) which is socialist-orientated and claims about 30,000 members, and the Confédération des Syndicats Chrêtiens (CLSC) which has about 10-12,000 members.

At the end of the War, there was a third communist-dominated organisation, which was dissolved in 1965/66. The CGT is divided into two main groups, one catering for miners and industrial workers generally and the other for railwaymen and transport workers and a small number of white-collar workers. There are also some independent unions, with very small memberships, catering for clerical workers, civil servants and local government employees. About 50 per cent of industrial workers belong to unions, but organisation is weak among salaried employees.

Despite the difference in their philosophy, the two main union bodies cooperate effectively vis-a-vis the employers, and have a joint committee for coordinating their policies.

Both sides of industry are represented in consultative bodies which deal with labour legislation.

Works councils

Works councils are compulsory by law in enterprises where there are more than 15 workers or 12 staff employees. Members are elected by all employees. They have mainly advisory functions — to advise on drafting and implementation of works rules, and on such matters as apprentice training and health and safety, and to conciliate in grievances.

8

The Netherlands

GENERAL

The Kingdom of the Netherlands covers an area of about 33,500 square kilometres and has a population of 13 million. It is about the most densely populated country in the world, with 356 inhabitants per square km. Nearly half the population lives in a narrow industrial strip extending between the ports of Rotterdam and Amsterdam. The birth rate is high and the death rate low, and the population is expected to go on rising. It is estimated that it will reach 14.5 million by 1980 and nearly 18 million by the year 2,000.

The Netherlands has common frontiers with Belgium and West Germany and a long seaboard. About a fifth of the territory is covered by water, but the Dutch, with their long experience of land reclamation, dike-building and dredging, have succeeded in harnessing water resources to the national development.

Traditionally an agricultural country, the Netherlands has, since the end of the War, developed an important and highly sophisticated industrial economy. The gross national product (1970) was over Fl 110,000 million, or nearly four times as much as in 1958. Of this, industry accounted for over 40 per cent, and agriculture for 7 per cent. National income per head has steadily risen.

The most important industries are engineering, chemicals, electronics, steel, food, drink and tobacco, textiles and building. The development of chemicals and petro-chemicals has been spectacular — the production index of chemicals increased (1963 = 100) to 259, and that of oil refineries to 201. The chemical industry manufactures about 2,000 different products.

There are few natural resources, apart from coal, which is being rapidly run down, and small quantities of oil. The discovery of natural gas in the northern provinces has led to revolutionary changes in both domestic and industrial energy consumption. A new aluminium plant has been built near the port of Delfzijl, in Groningen.

The Dutch have to import most of their raw materials and semi-finished products, and rely heavily on exports for their national wealth. About a quarter of their exports consist of agricultural products, and nearly two-thirds of finished manufactures, with chemical, electro-technical and metal goods leading the field.

International services (transport, shipping, insurance etc.) make an important contribution to the balance of payments.

The Netherlands is a constitutional monarchy, the Head of State being the hereditary sovereign. Parliament has two Houses, a lower Chamber with 150 representatives elected by universal suffrage on a proportional representation basis, and an Upper Chamber. Since the end of the War, the country has mainly been governed by Coalitions, dominated by the Christian-democratic bloc. The Socialist party is the main Opposition group. Until the summer of 1972 there was a Coalition, comprising the Catholic People's party, the People's Party for Freedom and Democracy, the Anti-revolutionary party, the Christian Industrial Union and the Democratic Socialist '70 (right-wing group) with 82 of the total number of seats.

Holland is divided into four regions — North, East, West and South, within which there are 11 provinces.

The Dutch economic policy is based on the principle of free competition and free private enterprise. The Government's role is regarded as being limited to creating a favourable climate for growth. But, on occasions, it will intervene in specific industries, eg the establishment of a wide strip rolling mill and the exploitation of natural gas.

It also plays a direct part in social policy and in the determination of wages (see p. 118).

The Netherlands' trade and prosperity is very much bound up with the European Economic Community, which has been an important factor in stimulating economic growth. The Dutch Government welcomes foreign investment. Between 1945 and 1971, no fewer than 1,029 foreign manufac-

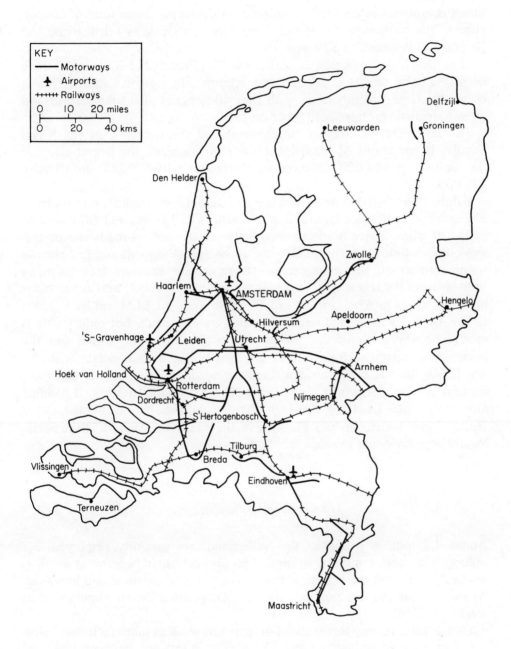

FIGURE 8.1   Major Centres and Communications

turing companies established subsidiaries or developed some form of cooperation in the Netherlands — 384 of these were American, 179 British and 153
German, 68 Belgian and 87 Swiss.

Most Dutch people speak English, as well as French and German, all three
languages being taught in post-primary schools. The Roman Catholic Church
claims the largest membership, with over 40 per cent of the population, and
other Calvinistic groups about 9 per cent.

The Hague is the seat of Government and the residence of the Royal
Family. It has about 564,000 inhabitants. Amsterdam, the largest city and
the capital, has 846,000, followed by Rotterdam with 699,000 and Utrecht,
276,000.

Within this small country, there are no internal communications problems.
The maximum distance from north to south is 230 miles, and from west to
east, 120 miles. There is an extensive network of modern roads and motorways, which link up with the German autobahns. Frequent and fast electric
trains connect all the main centres (there are for example four trains an
hour between the Hague and Amsterdam). Schiphol Airport, near Amsterdam,
links 101 cities in 69 countries and there are frequent KLM and BEA flights
to the United Kingdom. Freight is carried by air or rail, but bulk traffic is
mostly conveyed along the inland waterways. Both the Rhine and the
Meuse flow through Holland into the North Sea at Rotterdam with the
Scheldt to the south. Rotterdam claims to be the biggest, busiest and most
modern port in the world. Together with Amsterdam, in 1969, it handled
more cargo than Le Havre, Antwerp, Bremen and Hamburg combined. Other
Dutch ports, Terneuzen and Flushing in the south and Delfzijl in the north,
handle large sea-going vessels.

MANPOWER RESOURCES

About 4.7 million people in the Netherlands are gainfully employed, 3.7
million men and 1 million women. The proportion of women at work is
relatively low, and the tradition that women stay at home is still prevalent.
At the time of the last census, only 108,000 married Dutch women were at
work.

Of the total labour force, about 40 per cent work in manufacturing industry, 7 per cent in agriculture and 53 per cent in services. Between 1947 and
1969, the numbers engaged in agriculture fell by more than half and are
expected to decline still further during the 1970s. The breakdown of the

('000s)	1947	1969
Agriculture	770	340
Manufacturing	1,428	1,861
Mining	54	23
Chemicals and oil	44	115
Metal	370	556
Textiles, rubber, leather	303	205
Foodstuffs	187	203
Public utilities	30	43
Building	268	486
Services	1,668	2,424
Total	3,866	4,687

Source: Official Government Statistics

TABLE 8.2   Analysis of Employment by Sector

industrial labour force in Table 8.2 shows the development of various sectors since 1947.

Unemployment in the Netherlands has remained at a low level. Whereas before the War, about 14 per cent of the working population were out of work, the proportion between 1963 and 1969 averaged 1.6 per cent. During 1971 it averaged 1.6 per cent but by June 1972, it had risen to 2.6 per cent for men, and 1.5 per cent for women.

Despite the increase in unemployment, there is still an acute shortage of skilled labour, particularly in engineering and shipbuilding. This is partly attributable to the narrowness of the differential for skill which has been a feature of the Dutch labour market. The Government and both sides of industry attach increasing importance to the expansion of training. There are 25 Government vocational training centres, for adult workers, providing courses in building and engineering. Those who want training in other skills can receive this within industry and receive a training allowance from the Government.

A law was passed in 1970 to improve further education facilities for young people between 16 and 18 on a progressively rising scale. The whole system of training is now under review and its reform is being given high priority by industrial and education authorities.

The Netherlands

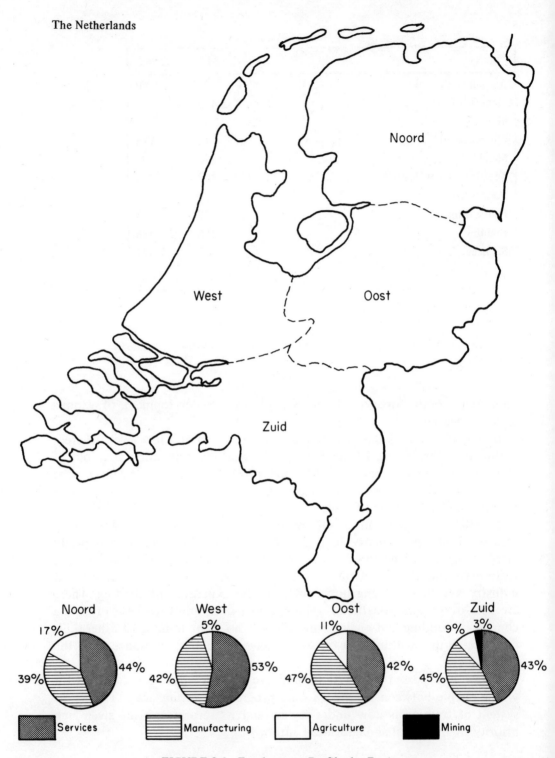

FIGURE 8.3   Employment Profiles by Region

Dutch employers, in common with those of other EEC countries, have been recruiting foreign workers to fill the manpower gap. In all about 100,000 European and Mediterranean migrants have settled in Holland, mainly from Greece, Spain, Portugal, Yugoslavia, Turkey and Morocco and the figure is expected to increase by about 15,000 entrants a year over the next four years. In addition there is a large entry of coloured workers from Surinam and the Antilles, who, as Dutch citizens, can enter freely. The migrants are concentrated in the big cities and industrial areas. Between 1945 and 1963, over 300,000 refugees and repatriates from Indonesia settled in the Netherlands.

The employers, trade unions and voluntary bodies have sought to achieve integration and to ease migrants' housing, education and general living problems. The main complaint of all immigrants is the high cost of accommodation. Nationals of non EEC countries are obliged to have a work permit, but they are employed on the same terms and conditions, and enjoy the same rights, as the Dutch.

Being a small and compact country, the Netherlands has not suffered from the same regional disparities as have France and Italy. The main problems have arisen from over-congestion in the industrial belt, based on Amsterdam, Rotterdam and Utrecht.

The employment profiles specific to each region are set out in Figure 8.3. It can be seen that agriculture plays a far more important role in the two northern areas.

There has been a steady drift of population from the agricultural areas of the north to the towns and industrial centres, and employment difficulties have arisen as a result of the decline of coal-mining in the south.

Per Cent	
West	0.7
Oost (and national average)	1.4
Zuid	2.0
Noord	2.9

Source: EEC

TABLE 8.4 Regional Unemployment Rates (1968)

The Dutch Government has given priority to regional development and has introduced a number of concessions for industries in the development areas which are mostly in the north and the extreme southwest. These include a capital grant of up to 25 per cent, based on the amount of factory floor space provided and a 50 per cent reduction in the purchase of land acquired for industrial development. Interest rate rebates are available in the provinces of Limburg and the northern provinces of Groningen, Friesland and Drenthe. Training and re-training facilities are being expanded in these areas. A flexible supplementary employment scheme of public works (land reclamation, roads etc.) is operated through the municipalities.

WAGES

There is a legal minimum wage which applies to all workers of 23 and over, and is adjusted annually on the basis of fluctuations in the general wage index. At the 1 July 1970, the minimum was 157,50 florins per week. By July 1972, it was 198.60 florins (for a five-day week). Over and above the minimum, wage rates are negotiated in industry by collective bargaining. Wages are paid weekly, or monthly, according to the contract of employment.

The average weekly gross earnings of industrial workers in October 1969 was 228.00 fl. Adding holiday and family allowances and allowing for deductions, this gave a net figure of 195.71 fl. The differentials for skill are narrower than in many EEC countries. The estimated figure for skilled workers (1969) was 230.50 florins; for semi-skilled, 215,50 florins; for unskilled 203.50 florins.

By April 1971, the average gross earnings figure had risen to 266.61 florins per week for men. Some examples for men in individual industries are set out in Table 8.5

Despite the provisions of the Treaty of Rome, there is a wide gap between men's and women's earnings. The average earned by all women in 1971 was 61 per cent of that of a male worker.

Office workers' salaries vary according to age and education. A survey in 1965 showed that a man of 35-40 with primary education earned about 10,907 florins a year, while a man of that age with higher education earned 27,299 florins. Women in the same age group earned from 8,247 to 19.250 florins a year. The survey was discontinued, but it is estimated that the salary index for men rose by 37 per cent between 1965 and 1970, and for women by 46 per cent. In January 1970, an unmarried clerk in the civil service averaged 7,386 florins a year and a top administrator 25,188 to 36,000 florins.

Although the wage index for agricultural workers more than doubled

Gross weekly rates 1971	
	Florins
Minerals	273.11
Foodstuffs	270.72
Textiles	243.31
Footwear	230.36
Furniture	250.69
Paper	276.64
Leather	244.13
Chemicals	268.17
Oil	349.27
Metallurgical	281.81
Electrotechnical	241.40
Transport equipment	270.99
Building	276.96

Source: VNO Kronik 1971

TABLE 8.5 Average Earnings in Selected Industries

during the 1960s, they still remain at the bottom of the list, with a gross weekly wage of 183.98 fl. for a 48.9 hour week.

The ten highest paid industries are: coal mining, oil, chemicals, iron and steel, synthetic fibres, glass, metal manufacturing, shipbuilding, non-ferrous metals manufacturing, rubber and plastics (in that order).

Between 1964 and 1970, men's earnings in all industry rose by 79 per cent, and women's earnings by 95 per cent. Despite this steep rise, (only exceeded within the EEC by Italy) Dutch workers are less well paid than the Germans, Luxembourgeois, British and Belgians.

The length of the working week, fixed by legislation, is 48 hours, but under collective agreements, it ranges from 40 to 43¾ hours. Actual average hours worked throughout industry in October 1970 were 44.3. Overtime is calculated on the basic hourly rate, with 25 per cent for the first two, and 50 per cent for subsequent hours.

Holiday entitlement is generous. The minimum vacation is three weeks, sometimes increased to three and a half by agreement, and there are seven public holidays (New Year, Easter Monday, Ascension Day, Whit Monday, Christmas and Boxing Day and The Queen's Birthday). The basis of holiday pay is average hourly earnings plus three weeks per year. In some industries, extra days are granted according to age and length of service.

SOCIAL SECURITY

The Dutch spend a higher proportion of GNP on social security and welfare than any of the Six — it was 19.1 per cent in 1970 — and total expenditure increased by 243 per cent between 1962 and 1970. The system is comprehensive and was coordinated and simplified in an Act of 1967. Benefits are provided for old age and survivors, sickness, maternity and disablement, industrial injury, unemployment and family allowances.

Administration is mainly in the hands of a Social Insurance Bank, which has 22 Labour Councils throughout the country; these include representatives of employers and workers. There are special schemes for civil servants and railwaymen.

The following table shows the various contributions to social security paid by the two sides of industry, as at January 1972.

Per Cent	Employer	Employee	Maximum
National insurance			
General Old Age Pensions	—	10.3	
General Widows & Orphans	—	—	
Pensions Act	—	1.6	F 21,150 p.a.
General Special Sickness	2	—	
General Children's Allowance	1.8	—	
Employee persons insurance			
Health insurance	6.3	1	F 108 per diem
Working incapacity	4.05	1.35	
Compulsory sick fund	4.10	4.10	F 61 per diem
Unemployment benefits	0.50	0.5(av)	F 108 per diem
Wage earners' children's allowances	3.13	—	F 21,150 p.a.

Source: Ministry of Social Affairs, The Hague.

TABLE 8.6 Contributions to Social Security

Sickness and disablement

Under the Health Insurance Act, sick pay benefits, amounting to 80 per cent of daily earnings, are paid on and after the third day for every day of illness up to a maximum of 52 weeks. Contributions towards cash benefits are paid for by the employer and vary in different industries, but employers and workers contribute equally towards medical benefits. Insured workers are entitled to medical, specialist and dental treatment, hospitalisation up to one year, medicines and such extras as artificial limbs. Special arrangements are made for meeting expenses for treatment in mental hospitals, psychiatric institutions and sanatoria.

Disabled people, under the Working Incapacity Act, are entitled to disability benefits, if after receiving health insurance benefits for 52 weeks, they are still at least 15 per cent incapacitated. These benefits amount to up to 80 per cent of the daily wage and are reduced in proportion to the degree of disablement.

Temporary disablement is covered by the sickness insurance scheme. Permanently disabled workers receive a pension at a percentage, varying according to the degree of disablement, provided this has been assessed at 15 per cent or more. Supplementary benefits include constant attendance allowance, where disablement is over 80 per cent and the same rates for widows' pensions as in the general widows' scheme.

Retirement and other pensions

The normal retiring age is 65 for both men and women. The maximum pension, at 1 July 1972, is Florins 5,364 per annum for a single person and Florins 7,596 for a married couple. Pensions are adjusted for every three per cent move in the wage index. Employees contribute 11.9 per cent of their insurable earnings up to a ceiling of Florins 21,150 a year.

Widows' pensions at Florins 5,070 per annum, increased if there are children, are paid to widows at the age of 40 and over. A reduced temporary allowance is paid for widows who are not eligible for the full pension. Orphans' pensions vary according to age from Florins 1,720—3,324 per annum.

Because of the longevity of the Dutch people, pensions constitute an increasing burden of expenditure. Taking 1957 as 100, the index rose to 470 for a single pensioner and 401 for a married couple, by February 1970.

There are a number of private pension plans on an industrial or company basis, usually administered through an insurance company. In 1968, about 1.25 million workers were covered by industrial schemes, and half a million by company schemes. Benefits vary but are usually about 60-70 per cent of average of final salary, and include provision for survivors.

Family and maternity allowances

There are two schemes of children's allowances. There is a general scheme which pays allowances to everybody from the third child onwards, and a wage-earners' scheme, which pays for the first and second children. The amounts payable in July 1972 are as follows:

– First child	Fl 164.58 per quarter
– Second and third	Fl 184.86 per quarter
– Fourth and fifth	Fl 247.26 per quarter
– Sixth and seventh	Fl 273.00 per quarter
– Eighth and subsequent	Fl 302.64 per quarter

For maternity, an insured woman receives a benefit equal to her full daily earnings for 12 weeks (six before and six after confinement). Maternity care is available whether the baby is born at home or in hospital. For women who are not insured there is a maternity grant.

Unemployment benefit

Unemployment benefits provide for 80 per cent of a worker's daily insurable earnings and last for 156 days in any one year. There is no waiting period.

Since 1965, national assistance payments are available for people who fall below a certain level. The scheme is administered through the municipalities and is paid for entirely out of public funds.

LABOUR RELATIONS AND PROCEDURES

The Ministry of Social Affairs is broadly responsible for manpower and employment policies and for the organisation of the labour market. Its Director-General of Manpower deals directly with matters involving employment exchanges, vocational training, foreign workers and regional policies. It runs a national employment service, with 11 district offices, 90 regional employment offices and 45 branch offices. Employers are not compelled to use the official employment exchanges (apart from the engagement of women in the peat and cigar industries). Every employer of more than 20 workers is expected to employ a proportion (1 in 50) of handicapped workers.

Recruitment and contract of employment

There is only one type of employment contract, without any distinction between manual and non-manual workers, and there is no legal form of labour contract. It is, however, normal for the employer to specify in writing such details as notice of termination, the nature of the job and pay conditions. Contracts for fixed periods are normally terminated on their expiry. Those for indefinite periods are terminated by notice (the minimum is equal to the length of time between two successive pay days up to a maximum of six weeks). Account is taken of age and length of service. The contract may provide for a trial period of not more than two months.

A worker who considers that his employer has prematurely broken a contract may have a right to damages or to compensation. The employer must obtain the agreement of the regional employment bureau for such a breach.

Individual employers are responsible for measures for the protection of their work force, according to a series of safety regulations, enforced by the Ministry's inspectorate. Increasing emphasis is being laid on prevention and the need to make workers safety-conscious. Many larger firms have appointed their own safety inspectors and established joint safety committees. An Act of 1959 makes it compulsory to establish industrial medical services in all firms with more than 750 workers, and in smaller factories where processes involve a risk to health.

Collective bargaining

Collective bargaining has been recognised in Dutch law since 1907 and still provides the basis for wage determination. There are about 2,000 collective contracts in force, and once an agreement has been concluded, it becomes legally binding throughout the industry to which it refers. Agreements are normally valid for one year, but there is a tendency towards longer periods, eg in Philips, the contract lasts for three years.

A minimum wage is fixed by law and since July 1970 has been adjusted regularly according to the wage index.

For some years, the Dutch Government operated a type of statutory incomes policy. Immediately after the War, it decided to centralise the process of wage-fixing, in order to curb inflation and to allow economic development to proceed smoothly. The Minister had the right to decide the appropriate wage level for all industries and to impose a uniform wage structure linking wage rates to a standard method of job evaluation and to the level of productivity. The Government operated through a special Board of Mediators, which consulted with the 'Foundation of Labour', a joint body of employers and the three main union federations. In 1950 a tripartite Social and Economic Council was set up, which took over the principal functions of evaluating economic data and suggesting rates of permissible wage rises.

The wage increases decided upon at national level had to be translated into collective agreements, and all new agreements had to be approved by the Industrial Disputes Tribunal (under the Extraordinary Employment Relations Decree).

In general, during the 1950s, both employers and unions accepted this centralised system as being in the national interest, but pressures developed during the 1960s, as both sides were anxious to regain their freedom of bargaining and to limit Government intervention. With full employment and labour shortages, the workers were able to exert pressure for higher wages and employers were usually only too ready to make concessions in order not to lose labour to other firms. The Government was gradually obliged to relax its grip, though it still regarded the containment of inflation as a high priority. The dam burst in 1963, when the metal workers (always the pace-setters) defied the Government's ruling and won increases above the standard set. This example was followed by other sections and 1964 saw a wage explosion, with a general increase of 16 per cent, and the virtual collapse of the official wages policy.

Despite this, however, collective bargaining in the Netherlands has remained centralised. Contracts are usually negotiated at national or industrial level and apply throughout the industry concerned. They deal not only with wages, but with holidays, hours, training and other matters.

The Social and Economic Council, a tripartite advisory body, plays an important role and regularly suggests a feasible level of increase in wages. These act as guidelines, rather than as directives. The Minister of Social Affairs is legally entitled under the Wages Determination Act of 1970 to intervene in collective agreements which he considers damaging to national interests, but in practice he is chary of using these powers which are strongly resisted by the unions. The Dutch Government is still seeking to develop procedures for voluntary agreement which will limit inflationary increases in wages and prices.

Several tendencies developed in the late 1960s and early 1970s which are worthy of note. One is the trend towards monthly payments, which are made through a bank or the giro system. Another is the gradual dropping of piece-rate systems and special incentive schemes. There is also a growing move towards plant bargaining, which is likely to spread, as industrial units increase in size through mergers.

In general, collective bargaining in the Netherlands is in a state of trans-ition. The strict wage regulating machinery of the immediate postwar period has disappeared, but full decentralisation has not yet taken its place.

The Government has retained a measure of control over prices and must give its consent before prices of such essential items as bread, milk, fuels, rates and electricity are raised. This control has not prevented the Dutch from experiencing the steepest relative price rises of any EEC country during the 1960s. Taking 1963 as 100, the price index rose to 136 in 1969, although prices in the Netherlands have remained lower than in many EEC countries. The index rose steeply to 151.7 in 1971 and 159 in February 1972.

As a result of the remarkable degree of cooperation between employers and unions, and their acceptance of the need for industrial peace and pros-perity, Holland remained virtually free of strikes during the years after the war. During the early 1960s, an annual average of only 16 working days per 1,000 workers was lost in disputes. In 1970, a new type of militancy emerged, which was part of a general wave of unrest. The trouble started in Rotterdam, where so-called 'koppelbazen' or contract workers were taken on at higher wages than permanently employed workers in the port. Strikes spread throughout the country and were only settled when the employers agreed to pay a lump sum of Fl 400 to each permanent worker. In fact, some two million employees, including civil servants, received this lump sum, however remote they were from the initial cause of the dispute. During 1970, 140 days were lost through strikes per 1,000 workers compared with only 10 in 1969.

There is no official conciliation or arbitration machinery in the Nether-lands, and disputes are settled through the normal Courts, most of which have judges who specialise in labour matters.

The unions are now pressing for the right to strike to be included in the Law and to have a new Code drawn up. A Bill to this effect has been laid before Parliament. They also want civil servants and public employees, including railwaymen, who are now debarred from striking, to have the right to take industrial action.

Trade unions and employers

The Dutch trade unions are organised on denominational lines. There are three main Federations, the biggest being the NVV, which is socialist-inclined and non-sectarian. It has about 600,000 members. The Federation of Catholic Trade Unions has 400,000 and the National Protestant Federation about 240,000. Not much more than 40-50 per cent of the workers belong to a union. This is partly due to the past divisions in the movement and partly to the fact that since all workers benefit by agreements reached between employers and unions, the advantages of membership are not immediately obvious.

Each Federation operates through industrial groups and has been closely associated with a particular political party or religious domination. These links have been loosening and in recent years, discussions have been held on unification. It has now been agreed between the NVV and the Catholics that a joint Federation should come into existence in 1973 — the Protestants were unwilling to join in a merger. Such a Federation would exert a much more powerful influence than the separate organisations. Dutch trade union leaders are not exclusively interested in wage bargaining, but want to exercise more influence in economic and social policies, and to secure more democracy in industrial life.

The biggest and most militant unions are the metal-workers (NVV) with 110,000 members and the Catholic building workers, with 80,000 members.

The employers became organised at a much later date than the workers. The most important and representative body is the VNO, which deals with commercial and industrial matters, and was formed by the merger of two separate organisations in 1968. The Catholic and Christian employers have their own organisation, the Netherlands Christian Employers' Federation. For bargaining and consultative purposes, the two bodies combine in a Council of Employers' Organisations. The VNO represents most of the large and medium-sized companies, including foreign-owned firms. There are, in addition, a number of trade associations.

Despite the growth of militancy among the trade unions, particularly marked in engineering, labour relations have remained friendly and both sides of industry have tended to band together against Government intervention. The Foundation of Labour is the principal forum for employer-union discussion, though it plays a less important role than it did in the days of compulsory wage-fixing. Both employers and unions cooperate in the Social and Economic Council set up in 1950. This is a tripartite body, and includes representatives of agricultural, banking, etc interests.

It has 45 members, who are appointed for two years, and who advise the Government on every aspect of economic and social policy. At industry level, there are joint industrial boards, which deal with such matters as wages, conditions of employment, training, productivity, etc. They represent the specific interests of each industry vis-a-vis the Government, but their decisions can, nominally, be overruled by the Government.

Works councils

Under the Works Councils Act of 1950, firms with more than 25 workers are required to set up works councils. There are no sanctions for failure to comply and building, ocean shipping, railways, mining and butchery were exempted. The councils' functions have been defined as to 'contribute as far as possible to the optimum functioning of the business while recognising the independent position of the owners'. The trade unions have not in the past been over-enthusiastic about works councils which they regard as organisations run on paternalistic lines. But a new law passed in January 1971 vests the councils with more authority. Whereas before the new Act members had the right to be informed about managerial decisions, they now have the right to be consulted before decisions are taken on such issues as working time, holidays, profits, pensions, safety and personnel policy.

As a result of the new law, union opposition has changed to full support and a determination to ensure that council members are equipped by training to play an effective part in discussions with management.

There is no equivalent in Dutch industry to the shop steward and hitherto union representation at factory level has been weak. In many engineering firms, the unions appoint a spokesman to take up workers' grievances and represent their interests, and this development is likely to spread.

Part Three

The Four

9

Denmark

GENERAL

The Kingdom of Denmark covers an area of about 43,000sq.km. It consists of the islands of Zeeland, Funen and Lolland, the peninsular of Jutland and the Island of Bornholm in the Baltic. It has only one land frontier to the south, where Jutland borders on the German province of Schleswig-Holstein. There are in all nearly 500 islands, of which 97 are inhabited. Greenland, with about 44,000 inhabitants and the Faroe islands, with about 37,000 are part of Denmark.

The total population is just under 5 million, and the density of population is 114 per square kilometre (excluding Greenland and the Faroes).

Gross national product in 1970 amounted to £6,500 million, of which 40.1 per cent of domestic sources was contributed by industry and 8.9 per cent by agriculture. The country experienced a very rapid rise in its GNP during the 1960s, but after mid-1970 there was a falling off in the previously high rate of expansion. In mid-1971 total output was estimated to be about 2 per cent higher than in the previous year.

Denmark is traditionally an agricultural country. Almost three-quarters of its territory is used for farming, market gardening and horticulture, but in recent years there has been a marked shift to industry in terms of both employment and output.

In 1970, the value of manufactured exports was about three times that of agricultural products. Denmark's main exports in the agricultural sector are dairy produce, bacon, meat, canned goods and fish products, and among industrial products, ships, machinery and equipment, as well as furniture, glass and other quality consumer products. In the first half of 1971 exports of machinery increased by 12 per cent, compared with an increase of 16 per cent between 1969 and 1970. This slowing-down is surprisingly attributed by the government partly to the 'persistent decline in exports of hair curlers'.

There are no raw materials of any significance and the Danes have to import supplies of fuel and raw materials for agriculture and industry, as well as feeding-stuffs and fertilisers, timber and steel. The country's main trade is with the other Scandinavian countries, West Germany, Eastern Europe and the United Kingdom. Trade policies are liberal and customs tariffs are low. Denmark became a member of EFTA in 1960 and first applied to join the EEC in 1962.

Foreign investments have been increasing and by the late 1960s totalled over five milliard kroner, of which half represented American capital interests.

The main industries are foods, clothing, furniture, paper, textiles, chemicals, glass, metal and electrical engineering, shipbuilding and transport equipment.

Danish industrial production is on a small scale basis. There are altogether 6,800 concerns and about a third of the industrial labour force are employed in firms with 100 workers or less. The majority of firms are privately owned. Cooperatives dominate the agricultural scene.

Denmark is a constitutional monarchy, the sovereign being Head of State. Executive power is exercised in the Cabinet through the Prime Minister. Parliament (Folketing) is one-chamber and consists of 179 members elected for four years on universal suffrage, including two representatives each from Greenland and the Faroes. The main political parties are the Social Democrats, Conservatives, Liberals, Radical Liberals and two splinter Socialist parties. Since September 1971 Denmark has been governed by a minority Social-Democrat Government. Parliament elects the Ombudsman, whose task it is to investigate complaints made by the public against Ministers and officials.

The country is divided, administratively, into 13 county districts and Copenhagen enjoys special status.

There is some public concern about the composition of the population.

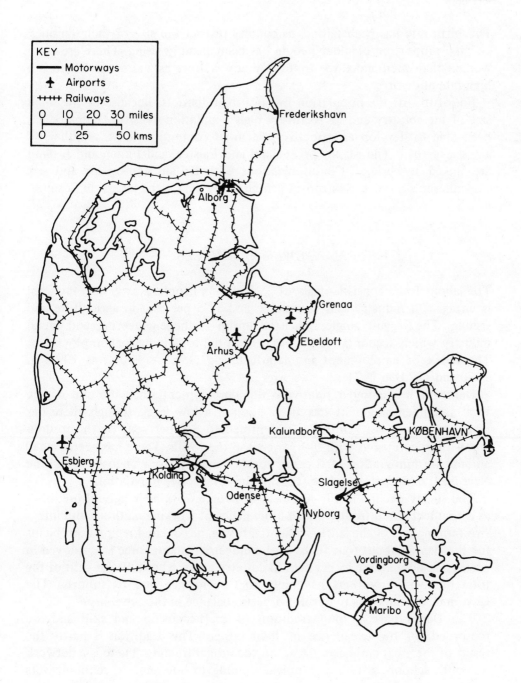

KEY
— Motorways
✈ Airports
++++ Railways

0   10   20   30 miles
0   25   50 kms

Frederikshavn

Ålborg

Grenaa

Ebeldoft

Århus

Kalundborg

KØBENHAVN

Esbjerg

Kolding

Slagelse

Odense

Nyborg

Vordingborg

Maribo

FIGURE 9.1   Major Centres and Communications

133

The birth rate has been falling, as couples restrict the size of their families, and the proportion of older people has been steadily rising. There are more women than men and three times as many widows as widowers. There is a high rate of divorce.

Four-fifths of the population live in urban districts. Because of the small size of the country and its relatively high population density, Denmark has been able to develop an effective system of communications, whether by air, sea or road. The islands of Zeeland and Falster, and Funen and Jutland are linked by bridge. Communications with Britain are by air and sea, Copenhagen's airport, Kastrup (15 minutes by car) is the largest in Scandinavia.

MANPOWER RESOURCES

The labour force consists of about 2.25 million people. Nearly half the total is engaged in industry and commerce and 11.5 per cent in agriculture and fishing. The biggest single industrial group is the engineering and metal industry which accounts for 25 per cent of the total industrial employment. The index of employment in manufacturing (1963 = 100) was 109.5 in 1970 and 107.0 in 1971.

Denmark has enjoyed relatively full employment since the end of the War, and unemployment has been kept at a low level, though there has recently been a rise. In 1971, it represented 3.8 per cent of the insured population, compared with 2-3 per cent in the 1960s. There has been a small amount of immigration of foreign workers, mainly from Yugoslavia and the Near East, representing 1.4 per cent of the total active population.

The steady decline in the numbers of people working in agriculture, both as a result of the introduction of more efficient working methods and intensive farming and of the shift to manufacturing, has created regional problems for the Danes. About four-fifths of the industrial labour force is employed in towns and only about 15 per cent in country areas. About 40 per cent of the total number of workers have jobs in Copenhagen and its suburbs. The Government is anxious to develop a better balance in the economy.

The Danes have a long tradition of craftsmanship and skill and are renowned for the excellence of their design. This tradition is partly the result of the great emphasis placed on vocational training. There is a network of youth schools, offering technical training to boy and girl school-leavers up to the age of 18.

There are also occupational training schemes for unskilled workers and a

number of high-level Technical Colleges. The whole system of apprenticeship is now under review with the aim of providing a graduated system
which will combine general education with specialist technical training. The
length of apprenticeship varies from three to four years from ages 15 to
18.

WAGES

Danish wage levels are among the highest in Europe and have experienced a
very rapid rate of growth. Table 2.4 (page 21) shows that real wages rose
more steeply than in any of the Ten apart from Italy. Average hourly
earnings (men and women) rose from 809 öre in 1963 to 1,958 öre
in August 1971. During 1970, the average hourly earnings of non-agricultural workers were 13 per cent above those of the previous year, and for
1971, they were expected to rise by 10 per cent. The rise was the result of
a number of factors, including the reduction of the working week, rises in
the cost of living and the wage drift (adjustments over and above the national
basic minima).

During 1970 average consumer prices rose by 6 per cent, but, though the
rate tailed off during 1971, it was expected to increase in 1972.

The general level of salaries is broadly related to the salaries of civil
servants, which rose by 5.6 per cent in 1969 and 8 per cent in 1970.

For 1972, the main emphasis is placed on raising the pay of lower wage
groups and controlling price and wage increases under the Prices and Profits
Act, introduced in 1971.

The length of the working week (1971) is 41¾ hours for a five-day week,
determined by collective agreement. Overtime is paid at 22 per cent on fixed
hourly amounts for the first two hours and 36 per cent for the third and
fourth, and 72 per cent for the fifth hour and over. There are 18 days
holidays, with ten public holidays.

SOCIAL SECURITY

In common with other Scandinavian countries, Denmark has developed a
comprehensive system of social security, which provides benefits for old
age, survivors, disability, family allowances, sickness, unemployment and
industrial injuries. In addition, there are very generous social State-aided
schemes for housing, health, old age, education and social welfare.

Sickness and disablement

Health insurance covers everybody over 16, irrespective of health, age or financial position. Each year, the Ministry of Social Affairs lays down a maximum figure corresponding to the average earnings of a skilled worker. Those who fall below this amount come in an 'A' group and those above it in a 'B' group. Both groups are entitled to free hospital treatment, home nursing and burial benefits. 'A' members are entitled to free medical attention and 'B' members may in certain cases have their expenses refunded. Daily cash allowances (Kr. 67.50 a day for single people in 1969) are paid in the event of sickness. Workers and employers contribute towards sick pay and the remainder is borne by the State.

In the field of public health, there are 'Special care' schemes, which provide treatment and nursing, assistance to the mentally sick and handicapped, the blind and the deaf, and children's welfare. There is legislation ensuring the care of old people and the chronic sick and providing home helps. People above the insurable limit can join 'continuation health insurance societies' for a variety of medical benefits.

Disability benefits, under the general scheme, are based on the extent of disablement and the employee's income. The full disability pension is Kr 19,668 per annum, and for disability of between half and two-thirds it is Kr 7,008 per annum. The pension is subject to a means test.

Under the Industrial Injuries Insurance Act, every employer is obliged to insure against accidents at work and occupational diseases. Treatment and cash allowances are provided.

Retirement and other pensions

As in Norway, there is a two-tier system of pensions, a general flat-rate scheme and a supplementary (ATP) scheme. Pensions are normally paid to men and women at 67. Employees contribute 4 per cent of taxable income towards the basic old age pension; employers do not contribute directly but pay Kr 21 a year per employee towards disability benefits.

Old age pensions are adjusted twice a year to take account of changes in the cost of living index. In October 1971 the pension amounted to Kr 9,264 per annum for a single person and Kr 13,956 for a married couple (wife being over 67). Single women are entitled to a pension subject to a means test.

Supplementary pensions are available to gainfully employed people, working at least 15 hours a week with the same employer payable at 67. From October 1972, contributions were increased to Kr 3.00 for employees and Kr 6.00 for employers (nearly double the previous rate) in order to provide for a new maximum pension of Kr 4,000 per annum plus a post-retirement bonus of 30 per cent.

Both types of pension contain provision for survivors. A widow over 55, or 45 if caring for two or more children under 18, is entitled to a pension equal to a single person's, subject to a means test. Under the supplementary scheme, a widow on her 62nd birthday is entitled, subject to ten years' contributions by her husband, to a pension equal to 50 per cent of the old age pension earned at the date of death of her husband.

A number of private companies operate pension plans. These are usually based on fixed contributions from both sides (ten per cent from the employer and five per cent from the employee) and pensions tend to be related to final salary, integration with the flat rate State pension being achieved by a salary offset in determining pensionable salary. Widows, orphans and disability pensions are usually included in these schemes.

Unemployment benefits

Unemployment benefit is administered by the government through the public labour exchanges and takes the form of daily cash allowances to the unemployed. There is a maximum sum of Kr 67.50 a day (1969). No unemployed worker may receive an allowance in excess of four-fifths of his previous wage.

The whole field of social security and social services is under constant review, with the object of improving standards and ensuring a better coordination between the various branches. Benefits are frequently revised in an upward direction, largely under pressure from the trade unions.

LABOUR RELATIONS AND PROCEDURES

Recruitment and contract of employment

As in all Scandinavia, there is a comprehensive system of labour legislation, with the Ministry of Labour as the authority for implementing it. Various Acts govern relationships between employers and workers, placement and unemployment insurance, vocational training, young workers, emigration, public works and finding work for the unemployed. Placement services are operated mainly by public labour exchanges, under a Directorate of Labour, which is also responsible for State youth industrial schools and for training semi-skilled workers. There are 29 offices with about 400 local branch offices.

Collective bargaining

Wages and salaries are determined by collective bargaining, which is legally required. There are nationwide negotiations between unions and employers, covering wages, hours and the settlement of disputes. These agreements usually last for a two year period though adjustments are made at half-yearly intervals in the light of movements in the cost of living index. Mediation and arbitration have an important place in collective bargaining. There is a Labour Court, whose decisions are binding and whose members are chosen by the two sides of industry. It has jurisdiction over breaches of contract and disputes over the legality of strikes and lock-outs. As in Norway, strikes are only allowed after established procedures for peaceful settlement and mediation have been exhausted.

The result of the legal framework is that there are relatively few stoppages of work in Denmark. Between 1961 and 1970, an average of 414 working days a year per 1,000 workers was lost in disputes, including major stoppages in 1961. In the three years 1966-1968, the average number of days lost was only 23, but the figure increased to 160 in 1970.

Trade unions and employers

Apart from the legal limitations, a prime cause of the small number of disputes is the harmonious relationship existing between employers and unions and the mutual desire to concentrate on improving living standards and national prosperity.

The employers are organised in an Association, which is a federation of industrial and regional bodies, as well as of individual firms. Its members employ about half the nation's wage and salary earners. A national agreement reached with the trade unions lays down the rights and duties of employers and unions, basic procedures for the peaceful settlement of disputes and the pattern of labour-management relations.

About 65 per cent of wage and salary earners belong to trade unions, most of which are affiliated to the Federation of Trade Unions (LO). There are 50 unions within LO and membership at the end of 1971 was 909,469 (650,843 men and 258,626 women). There are separate organisations for civil servants and salaried employees. The LO structure is centralised; workers are not organised on an industrial basis as in Norway but according to their occupation or trade.

Works councils

The employers and union central organisations reached a voluntary agreement in October 1970, setting out the principles and practices for cooperation and cooperation committees, replacing agreements on joint consultation made in 1947 and 1964. By 1971, 705 cooperation committees had been established, compared with 600 in 1968, and covered 80-85 per cent of industrial workers.*

The 1970 agreement, drawn up under union pressure, recognised the workers' right to 'co-determination' in matters involving local work organisation, safety and welfare and personnel policy, with 'co-influence' in production planning and changes in operation or within the company. 'Co-determination' is defined as 'an obligation to strive for agreement locally' while 'co-influence' provides the opportunity to exchange ideas and suggestions with a view to influencing management decisions. The committees are entitled to receive information about the company's finances and prospects, but wages are excluded from their scope. They consist of an equal number of management and workers' representatives, who are usually shop stewards. A joint Cooperation Board visits companies in order to check progress and stimulate participation.

There is also legal provision for joint safety committees in all enterprises employing over 10 workers.

At national level, employers and union leaders are represented on the Labour Market Council, which is a forum for discussion and information on labour-management relations and employment policies.

---

* Article on Joint consultation in Danish industry, by Erik Ohrt, 'Industrial Participation' Spring 1972.

139

10

The Republic of Ireland

GENERAL

The Republic of Ireland covers an area of 68,900 square kilometres and has 2,944,000 inhabitants (1970). Its density of population, 42 per sq.km, is one of the lowest in Europe.

Ireland is still basically an agricultural country. Farming and livestock account for about one-fifth of the national income, two-fifths of total exports and employ nearly a third of the working population. The family farm predominates and the average size of holding is 40 acres.

As well as seeking to improve the efficiency of agriculture, the Government has, since the late 1950s, been concerned to expand the nation's industrial base. Between 1960 and 1971 (estimated) gross output of all manufacturing industries rose from value £434 million to £1,195.3 million and the volume of exports from manufacturing rose from £83.8 million to £349 million. The manufacturing sector is still primarily concerned with the processing of agricultural and food products – bacon, meat, dairy products, grain milling and animal feeding stuffs, sugar and malting.

Many other industries, both traditional and new, have recently been developed, including clothing, textiles, metals, motor assembly and chemicals.

After the mid-1960s there was a rapid rise in gross national product from

141

£1,019,700 in 1965 to £1,677,000 in 1970 (market prices). In 1968 national production increased at a record rate of 8 per cent, but since then the rate has declined — to four per cent in 1969 and two and a half per cent in 1970, with the hope of some recovery in 1971/72. Tourism during the 1960s was one of the main sources of income, but owing to the political disturbances in the North, tourist receipts were expected to decline considerably.

One of the main reasons why the Irish are anxious to join the Common Market is to expand their markets abroad, regain their industrial momentum and avoid excessive dependence on the United Kingdom, which supplies Ireland with half its total imports and takes about two-thirds of its exports. The first application was made by the then Prime Minister, Mr Sean Lemass, in 1961. In May 1972 the Irish people voted overwhelmingly in favour of entry in a referendum — 83 per cent for and 17 per cent against.

Ireland has few natural resources and imports coal, oil and iron and steel, as well as agricultural and other machinery, vehicles, chemicals and consumer goods.

About half its exports in 1971 consisted of agricultural products (£221.2 million) while industrial exports accounted for £277 million. Apart from UK, its main trade was with the other EFTA and the EEC countries, and the USA.

Exploration is proceeding for minerals, including deposits of zinc, silver and copper. Full use has been made of peat resources, which account for about a quarter of electricity production, as well as for heating and horticultural purposes.

The Republic of Ireland, established as an independent nation after the Civil War of the 1920s, is a parliamentary democracy. It has two Houses of Parliament, the Dail, with 144 members and the Senate, with 60 members. The elected President, Mr De Valera, is Head of State and the Prime Minister is Head of Government — since 1966 Mr John Lynch, leader of the ruling Flanne Fail Party. A written Constitution was adopted in 1937 by plebiscite.

Irish is the national and official language, with English as the second language. Ninety-five per cent of the population are Roman Catholics. The 26 counties grouped in provinces comprise Munster (6), Leinster (12) and Connacht (5) with a small part of Ulster. Though the Republic has a free enterprise economy, the Government, after consultation with interested bodies, draws up periodic plans for economic expansion.

Public transport, road and rail, within the Republic is operated by a State Company, Aer Lingus and BEA run frequent services to and from the United Kingdom, and there are regular rail/sea connections. As well as the international airports at Dublin and Shannon, there is an airport at Cork, which

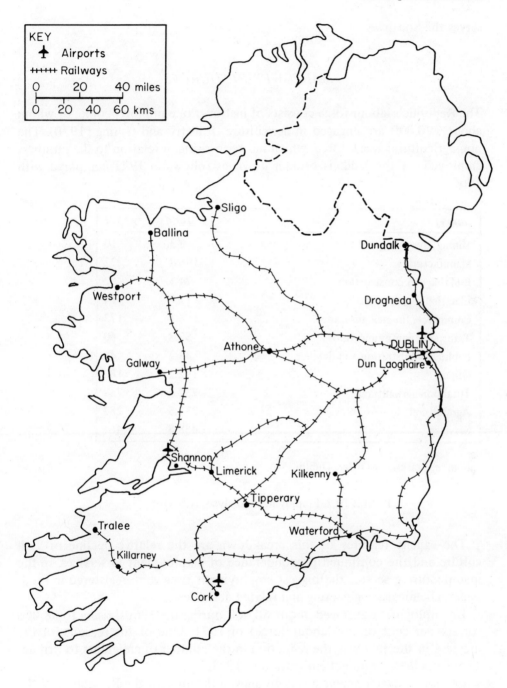

FIGURE 10.1   Major Centres and Communications

serves the South.

MANPOWER RESOURCES

The Republic's labour force consists of just over one million people, of whom about 290,000 are engaged in agriculture, forestry and fishing (1970). The non-agricultural work force, which has been rising in relation to the numbers employed on the land, is broken down as follows in 1971 compared with 1966.

(000's)	1966	1971
Mining, quarrying and turf	9.3	10
Manufacturing	198.4	222
Building and construction	74.1	82
Electricity, gas, water	11.9	14
Commerce, finance, insurance	166.1	173
Transport, communications	57.3	60
Public administration and defence	43.2	48
Other	172.2	180
Total non agricultural	732.5	789
Agricultural	333.5	282
Services	438.8	461

Source: Stationery Office, Dublin.

TABLE 10.2 Employment Analysis by Sector

The salient features of this breakdown are the relative decline of agriculture and the continued preponderance of employment in services. In the manufacturing sector, the biggest employment rises were registered in food, paper, chemicals, engineering and related activities.

Unemployment averaged about 60,000 during the 1960s, rising to 68,000 (or six per cent of the labour force) in 1971. One of the reasons for the increase in the rate was the reduction in the number of emigrants to Britain. There was little or no net emigration in 1971.

Economic development has been uneven throughout the Republic and the Government is seeking to secure a better balance, and bring more employment and better amenities to some of the depressed areas in the West and Southwest. These have been progressively depopulated and derive their main income from the tourist trade. A special regional development fund to help firms in the West was established in 1970/71.

At the end of 1969 the numbers of people on the live register (ie receiving unemployment benefit or unemployment assistance) varied in different regions. These substantial variations are set out in Table 10.3.

	Per Cent
Dublin/Dun Laoghaire	5.0
North Leinster	7.4
South Leinster	7.6
North Munster	8.2
South Munster	5.9
North Connacht	11.7
South Connacht	7.7
Ulster, part of	13.5
Republic of Ireland Average	6.5

Source: The trend of employment and unemployment
CSO, Dublin, November 1970.

TABLE 10.3   Regional Analysis of Unemployment

As part of its policy for achieving a better balance, the government provides substantial inducements for industrial investment. New manufacturing companies are exempt from taxes on profits derived from Irish-manufactured goods for ten years and those located at Shannon Industrial Estate enjoy total tax exemption until 1983. There is no capital gains tax. Grants, up to a maximum of two-thirds in the west, are made towards the cost of factory sites, buildings, machinery and equipment and towards the training of workers for new industries.

While the centre of industry and commerce remains in Dublin, the capital, industrial estates have been developed at Galway, Shannon and Waterford, where factories can be rented or built on favourable terms and where labour is readily available.

As a result of Government measures, there was an influx of foreign investment during the 1960s. Out of 273 projects established with foreign participation, Britain accounted for 40 per cent, Germany for 20 per cent, USA,

16 per cent, and Holland 5 per cent. Nearly every European country is represented on the list of foreign investors.

The majority of recruits to the newer industries come straight from villages and rural areas, and have no experience or industrial traditions. Crash programmes of on-the-job training have been introduced and training is being expanded as rapidly as possible. Most employers from abroad agree that they find the workers very adaptable and quick to learn new skills and trades.

Under the Industrial Training Act, a levy/grant system is designed to encourage in-plant training. Permanent training centres have been established at Dublin, Cork, Shannon, Galway and Waterford, as well as mobile centres in Athlone, Ballina and Tralee. By the end of 1972 it is planned to have a total training capacity of 1,200 places with an annual throughput of 2,200 trainees, and courses for 500 training instructors. Special training facilities have been organised for the hotel and catering trade and for the building industry.

There is a system of vocational schools giving general and practical training for employment to pupils who have left primary school, as well as adult evening courses. There are regional technical colleges in 9 centres.

The Irish Management Institute is primarily responsible for training executives. In 1971, over 5,000 managers took part in the institute's courses, and special workshop courses are being developed to help firms meet EEC conditions.

WAGES

Wage costs are considerably lower in Ireland than in other countries of the Ten, but the Republic has suffered from the effects of inflation.

Taking 1963 as 100, the index of average weekly earnings in industry rose by stages to 365.7 in September 1971. In 1965, the average earned in manufacturing was £10.84 and in September 1971, it was £21.08. During the same seven years the consumer price index increased from 112 (1963 = 100) to 158. The index of wage costs per unit of output between 1965 and September 1971 rose from 106 to 159 and the index of output per man-hour from 110 to 142.

The country has taken the first steps towards a voluntary incomes policy, in order to try and curb the inflationary trend. A National Pay Agreement, reached in December 1970, provides for a first phase increase of £2 per week for adult men for one year, and a second phase increase of 4 per cent plus a cost of living supplement to operate for six months. The Government has established a National Prices Commission to keep a check on prices. The length of the working week in 1972 averaged just over 42 hours. In engineering the standard of a 40 hour week was agreed by collective bargaining. Overtime is paid at 50 per cent per hour on the basic hourly rate. The Irish worker receives at least ten days paid holidays, plus five days according to service and age (negotiated), plus six public holidays.

SOCIAL SECURITY

The Irish social security system is on the lines of the British. Contributions and benefits are on a flat rate.

Insurance is compulsory for all manual workers between the ages of 16 and 70 and for non-manual workers up to a ceiling of £1,600 a year. Non-manual workers earning over this limit are allowed to continue as voluntary contributors for pensions.

The ordinary weekly rates of contribution for men from 4th October 1971 are £1.01 from the employer, £0.87 from the worker and for women £0.96 (employer) and £0.80 (worker).

Sickness and disablement

People in the lower income groups who cannot afford general practitioner services for themselves and their dependants are entitled to free general services, maternity and infant welfare, hospital and specialists, dental, ophthalmic and aural treatment (on production of a general medical services card issued by the appropriate regional Health Board). In their case the employer pays an additional health charge of £0.15.

Those with limited eligibility, ie middle income groups, themselves pay the £0.15 charge and are subject to a means test. They receive free maternity and infant care, hospital services and, in certain cases, drugs.

People in the higher income groups usually pay for their own medical treatment. Most health examinations and treatment are free for children. Tuberculosis and infectious disease services are available free to all.

The health services are operated by local authorities, mainly county councils, under the direction of the Minister of Health and costs are met from rates and taxes. The doctor/patient ratio at the end of 1969 was 102 per 100,000 population. Major hospital improvement and development

147

schemes are being put in train.

Apart from sickness, insured workers are entitled automatically under the insurance schemes to benefits covering unemployment, disability, invalidity, occupational injuries, marriage, maternity, widow's, orphan's, death, retirement, and treatment. In all cases, the insurance principle applies and benefits depend upon the requisite number of contributions having been paid.

Benefits were raised across the board from October 1972 and the new rates are quoted.

An employer is solely responsible for insuring workers against industrial accidents or disease, for all workers other than non-manual workers earning more than £1,600 per annum. The weekly contribution rate is 11p for a man and 8p for a woman. The occupational injuries scheme provides a range of benefits covering injury and disablement, unemployability supplement, constant attendance and hospital treatment allowances, and allowances for dependants, who also may qualify for death benefit.

Widows' contributory pensions provide an amount of £5.60, with £1.50 per child. The death grant is £25 for adults, £5 for a child under 5 and £15 for a child over 5.

Retirement and other pensions

Retirement pensions, payable at the age of 65-70 are £6.20 for a single person and £10.35 if there is an adult dependant.

There is a system of contributory old age pensions payable to an insured person at the age of 70. The personal rates are £6.20 a week between 70 and 80 and £6.70 for the over 80s.

Employees pay 87p a week (women 80p) and employers £1.01 for men and 96p for women.

Non-contributory old age pensions and widows' pensions are payable to people who do not qualify for contributory pensions, on the basis of a means test. In many cases, pensioners are entitled to free travel, electricity allowances, TV and radio.

For applicants with incomes below a certain limit, unemployment assistance is available, subject to a means test, and depending on family responsibilities.

Discussions are now in process about the introduction of pay-related benefits and about possible reforms in the various assistance schemes.

Family and maternity allowances

An insured woman can claim a marriage benefit, ranging from £3 to £10. There is a maternity grant of £4 and a maternity allowance of £5.55 for 12 weeks. Children's allowances are payable at the rate of 50p a month for the first, £1.50 a month for the second and £2.25 for each subsequent child. Normal age limit is 16.

Unemployment benefit

Unemployment benefit is paid to claimants who are capable of and available for work, under 70, and have not lost their job through misconduct or refused suitable work or training. The weekly rate is £5.55 with additions for dependants. The same benefit is paid in the case of disability benefit and invalidity pension. There is a redundancy scheme, comprising a lump sum and a series of weekly payments.

LABOUR RELATIONS AND PROCEDURES

The Department of Labour, set up in 1966, is responsible for operating a free employment exchange service, registering workers for unemployment insurance and assistance, and supervising the health insurance and assistance services. It also certifies trade unions and its Labour Inspectorate enforces the provisions of the Contracts of Employment Act, 1936, as amended.

Recruitment and contract of employment

The basis of employment is the contract of service between the individual employer and employee, which is legally enforceable. Only in rare cases are the terms of an individual contract explicitly set out. Normally these are determined by custom.

Collective bargaining

Wages and conditions of employment are generally fixed by collective bargaining. In agriculture, however, they are determined by a Wages Board and in a number of other low-paid industries (eg tobacco, hotels, hairdressing) there are joint labour committees, on the lines of the British Wages Councils, which lay down legal minimum wages.

The cornerstone of the Republic's Industrial relations system is the Labour Court, established in 1946. Under an independent chairman, it has 4-6 members, representing equally employers and workers. Though appointed by the Minister of Labour, the Court is an independent body.

Its main functions are to provide a conciliation service, investigate disputes, register agreements, establish joint labour committees, help the formation of joint industrial councils, make fair employment rules and fix standard wage rates for an area (non-binding).

The Court appoints conciliation officers, known as industrial relations officers. They do not exercise arbitration functions, but are frequently called in, on a voluntary and informal basis, to act as mediators. Each year about 500 disputes are referred to conciliation, and about three-quarters are settled. The officers also help with the establishment of procedure agreements for dealing with grievances, works councils, and general labour relations.

If requested by both parties or if it considers that there are exceptional circumstances, the Court can itself initiate investigations into disputes. Its recommendations are not legally binding. Of some 140 recommendations issued in 1968, over half were accepted. The Court can arbitrate or appoint an arbitrator if the two sides agree.

Under the Industrial Relations Acts, 1966 and 1969, there is provision for the registration of 'employment agreements'. Once registered these become legally binding. The Court has to be satisfied that there is genuine willingness on both sides to be registered, that the parties are substantially representative, that the agreement is not restrictive of employment or productivity and that there is an effective disputes procedure.

Both employers and union representatives have the right to complain to the Court if either party is in breach of a registered agreement, under penalty of a fine. Registration places certain limitations on the parties' freedom of action, but it does have the effect of discouraging industrial action. Unofficial strikes are illegal, and so are strikes to require changes by employers in a registered collective agreement.

Despite the elaborate procedural machinery, Ireland has been fairly strike-prone. Between 1961 and 1970 an average of 1,049 working days per 1,000 persons were lost through disputes. The year 1970 was particularly affected, with over 1 million working days lost, but there was an improvement in 1971, when the total was only 220,000. The improvement was in part attributed to the National Pay Agreement.

Trade unions and employers

The majority of employers belong to the Federated Union of Employers, which is the central negotiating organisation. There are a number of separate employers' organisations, eg in building, retail grocery, dairies, baking, but the FUE acts as the general spokesman vis-a-vis the government, advises its members on industrial relations and represents them in Labour Court procedures.

The Irish Congress of Trade Unions was formed in 1959, as a result of the merger between the Congress of Irish Unions and the Irish Trade Union Congress. It organises workers in both the Republic and Northern Ireland and is estimated to have about 450,000 members, of whom about 340,000 are in the Republic, organised in 88 registered unions (some of which are very small).

The multiplicity of unions is regarded as one of the weaknesses of the movement.

Just over half the workers are organised in craft, industrial or general unions. There are 7 general unions, of which the biggest is the Transport Union. As in Britain, the shop steward represents the interests of the workers at plant level. There are still a number of British-based unions operating in the Republic.

Works councils

There is no statutory provision for joint works councils, but these can be set up by mutual agreement, to discuss production and productivity issues.

11

Norway

GENERAL

Norway is the fifth largest country in Europe, covering 324,000 square kilometres, but with a population of only 3,888,305 (1971). Its density of population – 12.6 per square kilometre – is the lowest of the Ten. Nearly half the inhabitants live in rural districts and only about 3 per cent of the country is under cultivation. The economy is largely based on agriculture, forestry and fishing, although the direct contribution of these three groups to the Gross National Product declined during the 1960s from 14.1 per cent to about 6 per cent. Industry is primarily concerned with the manufacturing and processing of their products. Forests cover nearly a quarter of the land.

The country has extensive mineral resources, including pyrites, iron ore, limestone, quartz, dolomite and feldspar. Its most important asset, however, is the cheap and abundant supply of water power, which has been harnessed to electricity generation and forms the basis of the new electro-chemical and electro-metallurgical industries.

Norway has enjoyed steady economic growth since the end of the Second World War and has not suffered from stagnation or unemployment at any time. During the 1960s the GNP increased by 337 per cent at current prices or 113 per cent (allowing for inflation) and expansion continued during the first two years of the 1970s.

According to the OECD survey (January 1972) the rate of growth has been relatively steady and sufficiently high to keep output per employee and income per capita rising in line with developments in most European countries. It was also noted that the external financial position has been remarkably stable, with a good performance in exports which rose in value by 9.9 per cent during the 1960s.

The most important factor in Norway's external trade is the net earnings of shipping and the country is more dependent on shipping than any other in the world. Its merchant fleet totalled 19.7 million gross tons, representing about 9 per cent of world tonnage in 1971. Shipyards have been extensively modernised and are tending to produce larger and more specialised ships.

Ships and shipping apart, Norway's main exports are fish and fish preparations, pulp and paper, non ferrous metals, aluminium, steel, machinery and transport equipment. It imports cereals, fruit and other foods, ores and scrap, fuel and oil, chemicals, vehicles, machinery and consumer goods. Its main trade is with Sweden, the United Kingdom, West Germany, Denmark and the USA.

Norway is a constitutional monarchy. Its King is Head of State and executive power is vested in the Cabinet. Parliament (Storting) has 150 members, elected for four years on a universal suffrage. The main political parties are Labour, Conservative, Centre, Christian Democrats and Liberals. Labour held power from 1949 to 1963 and in March 1971 formed a minority Government.

As a largely social-democratic country, the main emphasis has been on measures to re-distribute wealth and expand the social services, especially housing and education. Norway has adopted a planned economy with broad output and social targets. However, it believes in a mixed economy and private enterprise accounts for nine-tenths of the numbers employed in industry. Production is on a small scale — nearly 70 per cent of its 18,200 industrial firms employ fewer than 10 people and contribute only 10 per cent to total output. At the other end of the scale, 270 companies and corporations have a workforce of 200 and over (electrochemicals, petroleum, shipbuilding, engineering and paper), and contribute nearly half the total value of output. The bulk of firms employ from 10-50 employees. Co-operatives play a considerable role in the economy.

The Government's main concern in recent years has been to develop the more remote areas and to encourage investment in their infrastructure. Owing to the vast distances and the topography, with the deep valleys, mountains, fjords and islands, transport and communications present a

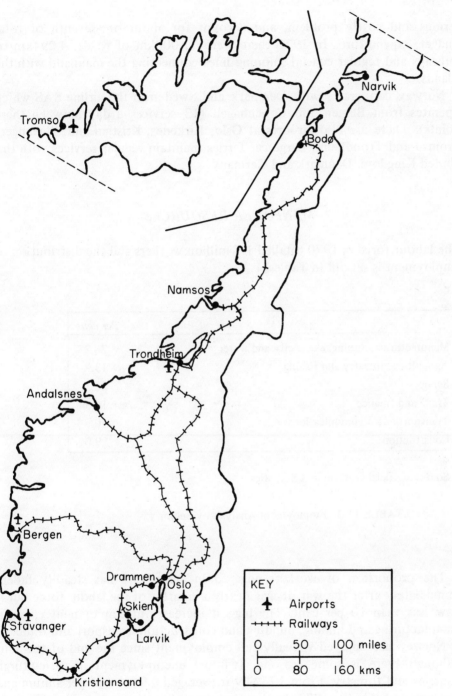

Norway

FIGURE 11.1   Major Centres and Communications

155

serious and costly problem, and account for about one-seventh of total budget expenditure. In 1971 there were 71,000km of roads, 4,294km of railways and regular coastal shipping lines connecting the mainland with the islands.

Norway cooperates with Denmark and Sweden in the airline SAS which operates from Bergen and Copenhagen (13 services a day between these points). There are also airports at Oslo, Kirkenes, Kristiansand, Stavanger, Tromso and Trondheim. Large car ferries maintain regular services with the United Kingdom, Denmark and Germany.

MANPOWER RESOURCES

The labour force in 1970 totalled 1.5 million workers and the distribution of employment is set out in Table 11.2.

	Per cent
Manufacturing, mining, electricity and water	28.2
Agriculture, forestry and fishing	13.9
Services	22.1
Trade and finance	16.3
Transport and communications	10.5
Construction	9.0

Source: Official Government Statistics

TABLE 11.2   Employment Analysis by Sector

The proportion of workers engaged in agriculture has steadily fallen. Immediately after the war, it was nearly a quarter of the labour force but is now less than 10 per cent. The biggest increases in employment came in manufacturing and mining, building and construction, transport and trade.

Norway has enjoyed virtually full employment since the end of the war, although there is some seasonal (winter) unemployment in agricultural, fisheries and forestry. From 1962-69 it averaged 0.9 per cent per annum and the level so far in the 1970s has hovered around the 1 per cent mark. Despite

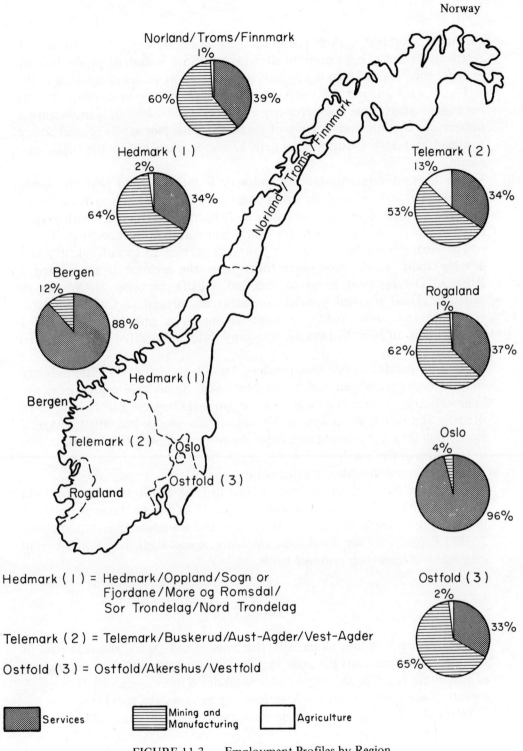

Norway

Norland/Troms/Finnmark
1%
60%   39%

Hedmark (I)
2%
64%   34%

Bergen
12%
88%

Telemark (2)
13%
53%   34%

Rogaland
1%
62%   37%

Oslo
4%
96%

Hedmark (I)

Bergen

Telemark (2)   Oslo

Rogaland   Ostfold (3)

Ostfold (3)
2%
65%   33%

Hedmark (I) = Hedmark/Oppland/Sogn or
              Fjordane/More og Romsdal/
              Sor Trondelag/Nord Trondelag

Telemark (2) = Telemark/Buskerud/Aust-Agder/Vest-Agder

Ostfold (3) = Ostfold/Akershus/Vestfold

Services   Mining and   Agriculture
            Manufacturing

FIGURE 11.3   Employment Profiles by Region

the acute shortage of skilled labour, there is hardly any immigration, and relatively little has been done to draw women into industrial production or increase their skills. There is a lack of suitable opportunities in light industry.

Figure 11.3 sets out the variations which exist in the employment profiles between regions. The low percentage of workers involved in manufacturing industry in the northern areas is of particular note. Norway's regional policy is aimed at taking industry to where labour is, rather than the other way round.

The heaviest concentration of industry is found in and near the larger coastal towns and cities of the south. More than half Norway's manufacturing industry is situated in Oslo and adjacent districts. Oslo, together with Bergen and Trondheim, provided work for nearly half a million workers in 1970.

The Government has pursued a policy of seeking to spread industry and develop more viable economies throughout the regions. It established a Regional Development Fund to this end. OECD commented: 'Norwegian agricultural and regional policies constitute an integral part of a long-term economic and social policy concept aiming at a smooth and balanced development of the Norwegian economy into a broadly-based industrial society'.

The four northern provinces, north of Trondheim, have very little industry and are under-populated and under-developed. Some large capital intensive hydro-electric, electro-chemical and electro-metallurgical plants have been sited in the north (including a big aluminium works beneath the Arctic circle) but they are capital-intensive and have not arrested the drift of labour to the cities of the south.

There are considerable disparities in income.

Taking the national average per income in 1968 as 100 the index for Oslo was 121, with 117 for Akerhus and 103 for Vestfold. In the four northern provinces it averaged 85. In the far north there is a minority group of about 20,000 Lapps, who live a nomadic existence, speak their own Finno-Ugrian language and tend their reindeer herds.

WAGES

Norwegian workers are, along with the Swedes and Danes, the best paid in Europe and labour costs per hour in industry (see Table 2.4) are the highest of any of the Ten. The shortage of skilled labour is one reason why Norwegian industrial workers have been able to force up earnings at a rapid rate.

Men's average hourly earnings in manufacturing rose from 7.77 kroner in

1963 to 15.51 kroner in mid-1971. The comparative figures for women were 5.40 kroner and 11.69 kroner. Building workers averaged 19.20 kroner an hour. Thus industrial earnings have more than doubled since 1963, whereas the consumer price index (1963 = 100) rose to 149.0.

About 50 per cent of wages are paid under piece-rates systems.

SOCIAL SECURITY

The Norwegian system of social security is comprehensive and generous. All residents are covered for old age, disability, unemployment, sickness, children's pensions, family allowances, and occupational injuries. In January 1967 a new Insurance Act was adopted, its chief feature being the introduction of an earnings-related element into pensions.

The costs of national insurance are met from employers' and workers' contributions. Employees now pay 4.5 per cent of salaries or wages, and employers 8.8 per cent.

The State and municipalities pay 4.5 per cent of pensionable income. It was estimated in the late 1960s that the employer's non wage expenditure, including fringe benefits, equalled 39 per cent of their wage bill for salaried employees and 28 per cent for hourly-paid workers.

There are reciprocal agreements with a number of countries, including the United Kingdom.

Sickness and disablement

Health insurance provides free medical care in hospitals and clinics, doctor's fees and free medicine in certain chronic illnesses. Cash benefits are paid during illness or pregnancy. Norway has one doctor per 630 inhabitants and one dentist per 1,251 inhabitants, and the emphasis in the medical system is on preventive medicine.

Pensions are available for disabled people between 18 and 70, provided they have sought rehabilitation for which a special allowance or grant is made. The amount is equivalent to the full old age pension provided the disability is over 50 per cent.

All workers are compulsorily insured against occupational injuries and industrial diseases, at the cost of the employers. Benefits include free medical treatment and financial support, according to the loss of earning capacity, and pensions for widows.

Retirement and other pensions

There is now a two-tier pension arrangement, comprising a basic and a supplementary pension. The basic pension is at a flat rate, fixed in January 1972 at Kr 7,900 and adjusted according to the cost and standard of living. A married couple receives 150 per cent of the basic amount and each dependent child under 18 a supplement of 25 per cent. The full pension is payable after 40 years contributions. The supplementary pension is calculated according to a complex system of pension 'points' which represent the ratio between the base amount and pensionable income. The full supplementary pension is equal to 45 per cent of pensionable income in excess of the basic amount.

A widow, under 70, will be entitled to the flat rate pension plus 55 per cent of the amount of the supplementary pension, on certain conditions and subject to her income. An orphan under 18 is entitled to 40 per cent of the basic amount, with 25 per cent for additional orphans, in the event of the loss of one parent. For the loss of both parents, the first child will receive full pension, the second 40 per cent of the basic amount and subsequent children 25 per cent each.

Unemployment benefit

Unemployment insurance comprises a cash allowance which varies according to income, with financial assistance for vocational training and re-settlement in another area.

LABOUR RELATIONS AND PROCEDURES

The Ministry of Local Government and Labour includes a Labour Department and a Regional Planning Department. The Labour Department is responsible for the Directorate of Manpower, which controls the employment exchange service and deals with matters relating to employment and unemployment.

Recruitment and contract of employment

The Ministry enforces and administers all labour laws. One of the most important of these is the Workers' Protection Act, 1936 as amended in 1956. This Act sets minimum standards for working conditions in industrial establishments, and regulates hours of work, overtime and night work, dismissal notices, the employment of women and children, and safety and health measures. Working conditions for seamen in the merchant marine and agricultural and domestic workers are regulated by a special law. Rules and regulations concerning safety at work and accident prevention are strictly enforced.

Collective bargaining

For most workers, wages and working conditions are determined by collective bargaining, usually on an industry-wide basis under rules established by a Basic Agreement, first negotiated in 1935 and periodically amended.

There is a National Wages Board, established by law in 1952 which monitors wage agreements throughout the country. This means that industrial workers have tended to receive commonly applied increases in wage rates.

A number of different payment systems operate in various industries.

In some cases, ie iron and metal working, hourly minima are laid down and workers can negotiate increases in their piece-rates. Elsewhere the standard wage, whose rate remains unchanged for the period of the contract, prevails. The latest development is the application of job evaluation in the larger companies. Here, workers are divided into grades with a single rate for each class. The most important national agreement covers about 50,000 iron and metal workers.

Most contracts stipulate that no alteration should be allowed for the duration of a contract, usually for two years. There is provision for adjustment if the cost of living changes. Stoppages are illegal during the duration of a contract.

Working hours are fixed by law at 42.5 per week and workers are legally entitled to four weeks holiday on full pay, plus ten public holidays. The five-day week is normal. Overtime rates in engineering are paid on a 42½ hour week at 40 per cent on the basic hourly rate for the first two and 50 per cent for subsequent hours.

The Norwegian system of conciliation and arbitration dates back to the 1915 Labour Disputes Act, when the Labour Court was set up and a system of mediation introduced. Its principles have remained virtually unchanged.

Two types of dispute are identified — those of 'right' and those of 'interest'. The former are disagreements about claims raised in connection with an existing collective contract; the latter are disputes over new wages or working conditions, ie new contracts. A dispute of right cannot be the subject of strike action but must be referred to the Labour Court, whose decisions are binding. Disputes of interest are referred to a State Mediator and if peace efforts fail, a stoppage is legitimate. The Labour Court has seven members, three independents including the chairman, and two nominated by employers and workers respectively. The State Mediator and his eight district mediators usually meet with a high degree of success in reconciliating the parties. There is a 'cooling off' period, in which the stoppage must be postponed until all conciliation efforts have been exhausted.

Compulsory arbitration was introduced after 1945 to ensure that the tasks of economic reconstruction would not be impeded by work stoppages, but arbitration is rarely used, and both employers and unions prefer to settle their differences on a voluntary basis.

The right to strike is a basic right, but Norway has comparatively few stoppages. Whereas in 1938, over half a million working days were lost through strikes, the figure did not exceed about 100,000 in the 1950s (except for 1956) and in 1964-65 totalled only 10,000. The average for the 1960s was 115 days lost per 1,000 employees.

Trade unions and employers

The central employers' organisation is the Norwegian Employers' Confederation (NAF) which has 9,300 members employing about 320,000 workers in manufacturing and inland transport. Its central Board, which exercises central and strict control over its members, is the policy-making body on labour and social matters and is responsible for national collective bargaining. Even employers' organisations outside NAF, in shipping, forestry and commerce, are influenced by its policies and guidelines. The parallel Federation of Norwegian Industries is concerned with trade and commercial affairs, but not with employment or industrial relations.

Norway is very highly unionised (about 70 per cent). The central body is the Federation of Trade Unions (LO) which organises about 580,000 members, or some 80 per cent of all trade unionists, in 43 national unions. It has close links with the Labour Party. With a highly centralised structure, LO wields great influence and discipline over affiliated unions.

White collar workers are represented within LO by a special Confederation (FSN) and outside it by the Central Committee of Salaried Employees. There are a number of other bodies, catering for engineers, civil servants, doctors, pharmacists and other professional groups.

Relations between NAF and LO are very close and the general climate is favourable to peace and productivity.

Works councils

In 1945 the two bodies agreed to set up joint production committees 'to promote the general well-being through cooperation and solidarity in industry'. These committees are obligatory in firms employing more than 50 workers and mandatory in smaller firms. Members are entitled to receive information about their firm's economic progress, deal with matters of safety, welfare and training and to be consulted about works rules, production methods, employment and redundancy, but not with wages or other matters within the scope of collective bargaining.

At plant level, the workers' spokesman is the shop steward, who is officially recognised in the Basic Agreement and wields considerable influence within the factory.

Despite the good relations between the two sides of industry, the State plays an important role in labour matters. There are tripartite Joint Industrial Councils which undertake planning, training and education activities and watch over progress of individual industries. The Labour directorate, concerned with employment policies, is tripartite, and workers' and employers' representatives are involved in committees dealing with labour legislation.

12

The United Kingdom

GENERAL

The United Kingdom of Great Britain and Northern Ireland is a constitutional monarchy, the hereditary sovereign being the Head of State. Parliament is composed of two Houses, the Commons, with 630 members and the Lords. Northern Ireland is represented in the House of Commons, but its own Parliament (Stormont) was suspended in 1971 because of the political crisis. There are three main political parties – the Conservatives, Labour and Liberals. In June 1970, the Conservatives formed the Government and the Labour Party, which had governed since 1964, became the official opposition. In the General Election, the Conservatives won 330 seats, Labour won 287 and the Liberals 6, the balance being made up of tiny independent and nationalist groups. There is no system of proportional representation in the UK. The Executive consists of the Cabinet, under the Prime Minister, and day-to-day administration is the responsibility of the civil service and the local authorities.

The United Kingdom covers an area of 244,956 square kilometres and has a total population of 55,346,551. Provisional figures for 1971 are set out in Table 12.1

	Area (sq km)	Population
England	130,868	45,870,062
Wales and Monmouthshire	20,841	2,723,596
Scotland	79,076	5,227,706
Northern Ireland	14,175	1,525,187

TABLE 12.1 Population by Country

The density of population is the fifth highest in the world, with 227 inhabitants per square kilometre, reaching as much as 322 per square kilometre in England and Wales. The population has grown by about five million during the past 20 years, as a result of the rise in the birth rate and the declining death rate. On the basis of these trends, it is expected to reach 58,885,000 in 1981 and 66,500,000 in 2001.

The age composition of the population shows a high proportion of the young and the old, and this imbalance is likely to persist into the 1980s.

In 1970, the gross national product was £42,819 million, of which over one-third was contributed by manufacturing industry and only three per cent by agriculture.

Until recently, coal was Britain's only major natural resource, but there are scattered deposits of low-grade iron ore. Natural gas was discovered in the North Sea in 1965 and oil in commercial quantities in 1970. The UK relies on imports for about half its consumption of foodstuffs and for nearly all its raw materials for industry. It is the world's third largest trading nation, takes nine per cent of the world's exports of primary products and provides 11 per cent of the world's exports of manufactured goods.

There was a balance of trade surplus of £979 million in 1971, when exports reached an all-time high level of £9,176 million and invisible exports totalled £5,192 million. The breakdown of exports and imports is set out in Table 12.2.

Within the engineering group, the leading industries were electrical machinery, ships, aircraft and cars.

The principal markets for UK exports are the USA, West Germany, the Irish Republic, EFTA, other EEC countries, as well as the Commonwealth. The six largest suppliers of imports are the USA, Canada, West Germany, the Netherlands, Sweden and France. Trade with other members of the Commonwealth and with the sterling area has tended to decline.

Economic growth has been slower in the UK than in any EEC country, as shown in Figure 2.2. Between 1965 and 1970, the annual volume growth of the GNP was 2.1 per cent, compared with 5.8 per cent for France, 4.5 per cent for Germany and 6 per cent for Italy. (OECD, December 1971.)

Per Cent by Value			
Exports		*Imports*	
Engineering products	43.5	Food, drink and tobacco	22.7
Metals	11.9	Mineral fuels and lubricants	10.5
Chemicals	9.7	Semi-manufactures	27.8
Food, drink and tobacco	6.4	Finished manufactures	22.7
Coal and petroleum products	2.6	Basic materials	15.2
Other manufactures	14.4	Miscellaneous	1.1
Textiles	4.9		
Other products	6.6		

Source: 'Britain 1972', Central Office of Information, HMSO 1971.

TABLE 12.2   Analysis of Foreign Trade (1970)

As in all European countries, the industrial pattern has changed since the end of the War. The traditional industries, such as coal and textiles, have declined — although coal still supplies nearly half the country's energy requirements. Some industries, especially those producing technologically advanced and rapidly developing products, have expanded — for example, computers, office machinery, scientific instruments, petro-chemicals, aircraft and aircraft engines. There has been a rapid rise in the consumption of oil and natural gas.

Britain spends over £1,000 million a year (2.7 per cent of its GNP) on scientific research and development. Nearly half of the total is financed by the government.

The British economy is 'mixed'. Nationalised industries include coal, rail transport, civil aviation, steel, electricity and gas, and are administered by public corporations. In some cases, eg civil aviation, independent companies compete with State corporations. In others (eg British Petroleum Ltd) the government holds shares.

Manufacturing is generally in the hands of private enterprise. The trend towards mergers and re-groupings developed rapidly during the 1960s, especially in the modern growth industries, such as car manufacture, electronics and electrical engineering. Many firms in the traditional sectors, such as ship-building and textiles, were merged or re-grouped in order, among other

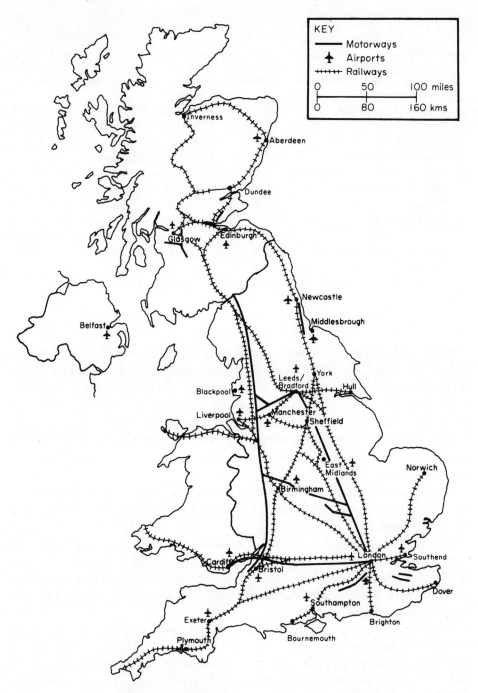

FIGURE 12.3   Major Centres and Communications

reasons, to present a stronger front against overseas competition. According to the latest census returns, the hundred largest enterprises, each with over 10,000 workers, account for about a third of total employment and net output, although the continuing significance of the small firm sector is reflected in the fact that a fifth of these totals is contributed by 60,000 enterprises with up to 100 employees.

As an island, the United Kingdom is heavily dependent on its shipping industry. During the 1960s, it embarked on a programme of modernising and deepening many of its ports and equipping them with improved cargo-handling facilities. Internal transport is by rail and road, and the canals play a very small part. The British Transport Board has aimed at improving both passenger and freight services, concentrating on fewer and better equipped marshalling yards and terminals for the through carriage of freight. The motor car 'explosion' has placed a severe strain on the country's road system, particularly in towns.

In June 1971, there were 334,743 kilometres of public highways, including about 1,600 km of motorways. Spending on new and better roads was estimated at over £470 million in 1971-2.

The British Airports Authority is responsible for London (Heathrow), Gatwick, Prestwick, Stansted (Essex) and Edinburgh airports. Air traffic has been increasing at a rapid rate – by 1970, 21.7 million passengers entered or left the country by air, compared with 2.5 million in 1955. The main State airlines, British Overseas Airways Corporation and British European Airways Corporation are to be merged administratively.

MANPOWER RESOURCES

In December 1971 the total working population of Great Britain was about 24,867,000, (15,934,000 men and 8,914,000 women). Of this total, 21,884,000 were employed persons, (13,482,000 men and 8,401,000 women).

The following table shows the breakdown by certain occupations in June 1960 and June 1971. It indicates the rundown of the labour force in agriculture, mining, textiles and shipbuilding, and the growth of the numbers employed in services, commerce and professional activities. It should, however, be pointed out that the industrial classification of many establishments was adjusted between June 1966 and June 1967, and that a revised basis of calculation was introduced after June 1964. The estimates are therefore not strictly comparable.

169

Employment (000s)	June 1960	June 1971
Agriculture, forestry and fishing	595.8	344.5
Mining and quarrying	766.0	401.3
Food, drink and tobacco	788.1	837.4
Coal and petroleum ⎤	528.6	57.6
Chemicals and allied ⎦		466.1
Metal manufacture	616.6	554.8
Mechanical engineering ⎤	2,029.2	1,142.3
Electrical engineering ⎦		880.5
Shipbuilding	2,253.3	191.8
Vehicles	911.8	812.9
Textiles	840.9	612.3
Clothing and footwear	565.3	472.8
Timber, furniture	288.5	293.3
Paper, printing and publishing	597.1	617.8
Other manufacturing	300.5	343.6
Building	1,422.7	1,248.6
Gas, electricity, water	370.9	368.8
Transport and communications	1,633.6	1,564.0
Distribution	2,773.6	2,582.0
Insurance, banking etc	538.1	971.3
Professional and scientific	1,937.0	2,903.8
Miscellaneous services	1,965.1	1,794.0
Public administration and defence	1,251.7	1,416.3
TOTAL All	22,036.0	22,027.0
TOTAL Manufacturing	8,662.9	8,431.6

Source: Department of Employment Gazette June 1972.

TABLE 12.4   Analysis of Employment by Sector 1960 and 1971

Figure 12.5 provides a further employment analysis by sector highlighting the variations in profiles between the economic planning regions.

At the end of the War, a number of Poles, Yugoslavs and Ukranians entered Britain where they settled down fairly easily. There are estimated to be about 800,000 coloured workers from the West Indies, India and Pakistan, who with their families total about 1½ million people or 2½ per cent of the population. The majority arrived before immigration controls were introduced and obliged them to obtain work permits.

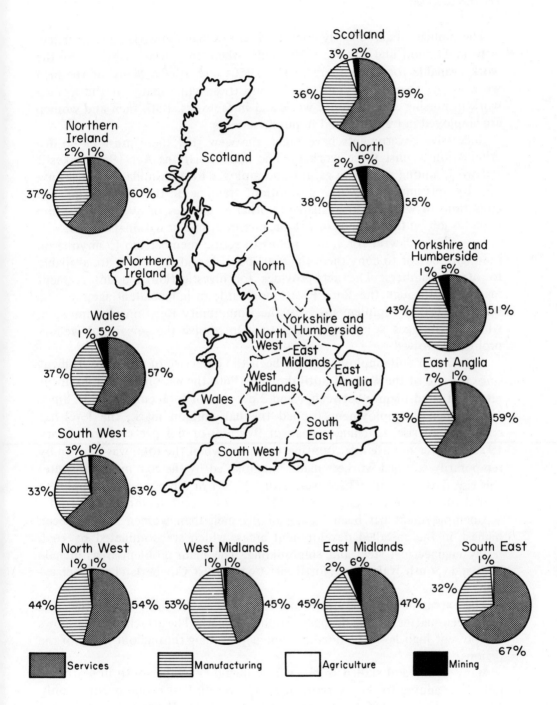

FIGURE 12.5   Employment Profiles by Region

171

The immigrants are mainly concentrated in urban industrial areas, particularly in London and the West Midlands, where they were attracted by the work available for them there in the 1950s and 1960s. Many of the men work in the engineering and textile industries, while many of the women work in nursing and domestic work and in factories. Both men and women are employed in transport and in public services.

Successive governments have taken the view that there must be no discrimination against these workers. The Race Relations Act 1968 makes it unlawful, among other things, for an employer to discriminate against anyone by refusing him work, promotion, training or the same terms and conditions of work as are available to other employees, or by dismissing him from his job on the grounds of colour, race or ethnic or national origins.

It is also unlawful for trade unions to refuse membership to anyone on these grounds or to deny them the same benefits and services as are available to other members. The act provides for investigation and enforcement machinery through the Race Relations Board, an independent agency. The Board's work is complemented by the Community Relations Commission, which encourages voluntary action to help resolve the social and welfare problems involved.

A policy of full employment has been the objective of every government since the end of the War and until the mid-1960s the national unemployment rate fluctuated mainly between 1 and 2 per cent of total employment. Since 1967, when unemployment topped the half million mark, the level has continued to rise, reaching a peak of 977,600 or 4.3 per cent in January 1972. In later months (discounting February when the total was swollen by temporarily stopped workers made unemployed by the coal mining dispute) this rise flattened out. There were still 822,861 or 3.6 per cent unemployed in mid-July in Great Britain and 45,335 or 8.7 per cent in Northern Ireland.

Unemployment has been higher among men than women and has been highest in the so-called development areas, which are dominated by coal, heavy engineering, steel and shipbuilding. The main problem areas include Scotland, South Wales, the North-east Coast, West Cumberland and Merseyside.

The extent of unemployment and the existence of these vulnerable areas have been matters of the deepest national concern. The attached table shows the present high levels of unemployment prevailing throughout many of the regions.

Many young and skilled workers have migrated to the south in search of jobs, thus adding to the overcrowding. The South East region occupies only 11 per cent of the UK total land area, but contains 31 per cent of the total

172

	Percentage as at 10th July 1972
South East	1.9
East Anglia	2.5
South West	3.2
West Midlands	3.7
East Midlands	3.0
Yorkshire and Humberside	4.0
North West	4.8
North	6.0
Wales	5.3
Scotland	6.5
Great Britain	3.6
Northern Ireland	9.2 *

Source: Department of Employment Gazette.

* at July 1972

TABLE 12.6 Regional Unemployment Rates

population. The Greater London Council and the outer metropolitan area together have about 13 million inhabitants, making it by far the largest urban concentration in Western Europe.

Every government, since the end of the War, has sought to limit the congestion in the south and divert firms to the development areas, through a dual system of controls and incentives. This policy takes several forms and three separate types of development area are identified:

Development areas — regions of generally high unemployment, as a result of the decline of traditional industries

Special development areas — within these regions where there has been excessive and prolonged unemployment, and

Intermediate areas — which have not shared in the prosperity of the main growth areas of the UK.

The level of assistance depends, in each case, on the severity of the unemployment problem.

The government operates a system in areas other than the development and special development areas whereby all industrial development above 15,000 square feet (10,000 square feet in the South East) requires an industrial development certificate. These certificates are widely available in the

173

intermediate areas, but in the Midlands and South East they are usually only granted when the government is satisfied that the project could not reasonably be undertaken in one of the areas of greater need.

Under the Industry Act 1972, a wide range of incentives are made available to all enterprises, whether they are British or from overseas. These include regional development grants for capital expenditure on new buildings and works, the adaptation of existing buildings and the provision of plant and machinery, in premises used wholly or mainly for qualifying activities — principally manufacturing, construction and mining. The rates of grant are 20 per cent in the development areas, and 22 per cent in the special development areas (except for construction industry plant used outside qualifying premises). In the intermediate areas, the grant at 20 per cent is not available for mining works. The grants will be made in respect of expenditure incurred on or after 22nd March 1972, (provided that the plant, machinery or mining works was not provided or building work begun before that date).

The Industry Act also empowers the Industrial Development Executive to help industry through selective assistance. New regional offices have been established in the assisted areas, and they are authorised to give selective financial assistance to encourage investment which promotes employment and modernisation. Such assistance can also be given outside these areas where it is likely to benefit the UK economy.

As an alternative to a building grant, firms may choose a two-year rent-free period in a Department of Trade and Industry factory.

A system of regional employment premiums operates in the development areas. Manufacturing employers receive premiums of £1.50 a week for each man employed, with lower rates for women and young persons. This system is to be phased out after September 1974.

Grants are available towards the cost of training in assisted areas. These are at the rate of £15 per week for men, with lower rates for women and young persons. Grants are also available towards the cost of transferring workers.

Over and above the financial incentives, firms in the assisted areas can benefit from the countrywide taxation allowances on capital expenditure. There is a first year allowance of 100 per cent on all new and second-hand plant and machinery (other than passenger cars) and an initial allowance of 40 per cent, and a 4 per cent per annum writing-down allowance on new industrial buildings and structures.

Northern Ireland has its own system of financial incentives, which is in certain respects more generous than that of the UK.

All assisted areas benefit by the arrangements for making grants to local authorities to enable them to improve the economic infra-structure (eg roads, drainage, hospitals, schools) and for clearing industrially derelict sites. The government also operates an Urban Programme, designed to help areas with particular severe social needs, such as inadequate housing, schools and other forms of deprivation.

Britain has a long-standing tradition of industrial skill and craftsmanship, particularly in the engineering, shipbuilding and printing industries. But the pattern of industry has been changing, with the decline of the older industries and the growth of modern, sophisticated and mass production techniques. The time-honoured system of apprenticeship has not produced enough skilled workers to meet industry's needs and has tended to be over-rigid and restrictive. A change in attitudes towards industrial training was brought about, following the publication of the Carr report on Training for Skill in 1962, which culminated in the Industrial Training Act of 1964. This act empowers the Employment Minister to set up training boards to guide employers on the length, nature and content of courses and to stimulate the spreading of schemes throughout each industry.

By mid-1971 there were 28 boards in existence, covering industries with over 15 million workers. The boards are financed by a levy on employers and pay grants to employers whose training arrangements reach an approved standard. A Central Training Council, composed of employers, trade union and educational representatives, advises the government on all aspects of industrial training.

The government has also expanded its direct role in vocational training. There are about 52 training centres, with a total of 11,000 places. About 18,400 men and women were trained in 1971. The majority of courses are in engineering and building, but arrangements have been made (August 1972) for training to be given in commercial, professional and clerical skills through Colleges of Further Education and private establishments. Training is provided mainly for younger workers, but courses are available for the unemployed, the disabled, ex-Service personnel and people who want to change their jobs. Allowances are paid during training.

The bulk of industrial training, however, is the direct responsibility of industry itself. The government has suggested (1972) the establishment of a National Training Agency, which would co-ordinate the work of the Industrial training boards, set standards and develop a national advisory service, paying particular attention to the training of managerial and supervisory staffs.

WAGES

Wages have been rising in the United Kingdom at a rate which has given rise to considerable concern, as increases in earnings have far outstripped rises in productivity. Output per person employed in manufacturing rose slowly during the 1960s, but improved in 1970-1 from 1.5 per cent in 1969 to 3.2 per cent in the first half of 1971. The index of labour costs in manufacturing (1963 = 100) rose to 132.3 per unit of output.

At the end of June 1972, the index of basic weekly rates stood at 248.2 (January 1956 = 100), representing an increase of 12.3 per cent over June 1971. (The indices of basic rates are based on the recognised minimum rates and do not reflect changes in earnings or in hours worked.) The index of average earnings for all employees for all industries and services was 130.4 in May 1972 (January 1970 = 100) an increase of 11.6 per cent over May 1971. In October 1971, average weekly earnings in manufacturing were £31.37 for men and £15.80 for women.

In October 1970, the index of average weekly earnings rose to 260 from a base figure of 100 in 1955. Taking 1962 as 100, the retail price index rose to 162.2 by May 1972, the biggest increases being in housing, fuel and light, and services.

The ten top industries for earnings (October 1970) were printing and publishing, tractor manufacturing, port transport, air transport, motor vehicle manufacturing, aircraft, sugar, synthetic fibres, photographic equipment and general chemicals.

The following table sets out the average weekly earnings of men and women in October 1971:

Table 12.7 shows the extent of the gap between male and female earnings. The difference is appreciably greater than in most EEC countries (see Table 2.5). In many industries, arrangements have been made to accelerate the women's rate of increase. Full implementation of the Equal Pay Act 1970 will be required by 29 December 1975.

Substantial variations also exist in earnings between regions. Table 12.8 shows the high rates of average earnings in the South East and West Midlands in contrast to the lower levels in the North, Scotland, Wales and Northern Ireland.

Industrial workers are normally paid by the week, and in cash, while salaried staffs are paid by the month. Over one million manual workers are now receiving their pay in forms other than cash, and this trend is likely to continue and become more acceptable both to workers and employers in terms of cost savings and security.

Sector	Men	Women
Food, Drinks and Tobacco	31.60	16.65
Coal and Petroleum	34.15	17.80
Chemicals and Allied	32.73	16.41
Metal Manufacture	31.67	15.18
Mechanical Engineering	29.84	17.18
Electrical Engineering	30.12	16.55
Shipbuilding	33.13	17.23
Vehicles	35.21	19.70
Textiles	28.02	15.09
Leather	26.56	13.64
Clothing and Footwear	26.00	14.53
Timber and Furniture	29.25	17.06
Paper and Printing	36.04	17.10
All Manufacturing	31.37	15.80
Building	30.11	13.42
Gas, Electricity and Water	30.74	16.88
Transport and Communications	33.73	22.32
Public Administration	24.51	17.57
All industries	30.93	15.80

Source: Department of Employment Gazette

TABLE 12.7 Average Earnings by Sector

Working hours are normally determined by collective bargaining, with the 40 hour, five day week as the standard. The average actually worked by manual workers in all manufacturing industries in October 1971 was 43.6 (men) and 37.5 (women) and in April 1971 by staff workers 38.7 (men) and 36.9 (women). Overtime is calculated on the basis of the minimum time rate plus 33.3 per cent for the first two and 50 per cent for subsequent hours.

British workers enjoy fewer holidays than those in the EEC, in 1972 the minimum length was two weeks, with six public holidays (Good Friday, Easter Monday, Spring and Summer Bank Holidays, Christmas and Boxing Day, with New Year's Day in Scotland). Many agreements provide for three weeks holiday and also for extra days according to length of service and status. Holiday pay is normally calculated on the basis of the time rate plus one-third.

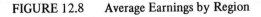

FIGURE 12.8   Average Earnings by Region

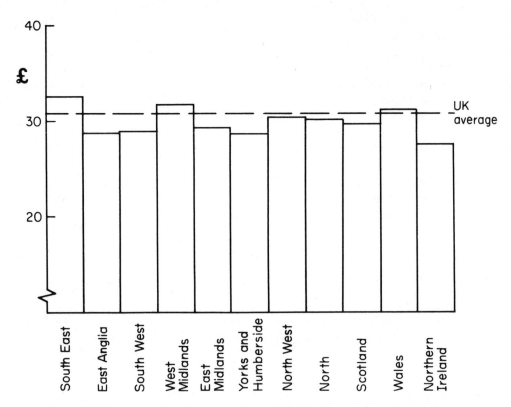

SOCIAL SECURITY

There are fewer 'fringe' benefits in the UK than in EEC countries. In all the Six, costs other than cash payments to employees range from 18 to 30 per cent, compared with 9 per cent in Britain. National expenditure on social welfare and security in 1970 represented 15.2 per cent of the GNP, compared with an average of over 16 per cent in the EEC. Against this must be set the advantages of the mainly free National Health Services, the cost of which is met overwhelmingly out of general taxation.

Britain's national social security system, which was revised by the Beveridge Committee in the early 1940s, came into force in July 1948 and its fundamental basis has remained unchanged. Benefits, which depend on a certain number of contributions having been paid, include sickness, maternity, survivors, industrial injuries, family allowances, retirement pensions and unemployment. Unlike most EEC countries, contributions and benefits are on a flat rate, though an element of supplementary earnings-related benefits has been introduced.

The scheme is operated by the Department of Health and Social Security, which has about 1,000 branch offices in the UK. Contributions are paid by means of stamps affixed to an insurance card.

There are three classes of insured persons, namely:

Class 1 employed people who work for an employer under contract of service − over 23 million

Class 2 self-employed people who total about 1½ million

Class 3 registered unemployed workers.

All three classes pay flat rate contributions. Men in Class 1 pay 0.88p a week and women 0.75, while the employer pays 2.15p and 1.40p for men and women respectively.

Graduated contributions are payable by employed people earning more than £9 a week, and provide a graduated addition to the retirement pension, and the earnings-related supplements to sickness, unemployment and widow's benefits. Contributions, the same for employers and employees, range from £0.01 to £1.47 a week.

Sickness and disablement

All employed and self-employed people are entitled to a flat rate benefit of £6 a week, plus allowances for dependants (£3.70 for a wife). There are three waiting days. Under the earnings-related supplement scheme, available for people who earned a minimum of £450 in the relevant tax year, there are 12 waiting days, with a maximum benefit of 85 per cent of average weekly earnings up to 156 days.

The State pays 25 per cent of national insurance contribution and $33\frac{1}{3}$ per cent of self-employed contributions. Medical benefits are available under the National Health Service, which includes general practitioner and specialist treatment, dental and eye treatment, hospitalisation and rehabilitation. Certain charges, eg prescriptions, dentures and spectacles are made, with some exceptions for children and pensioners.

A scheme covering industrial injuries and illnesses came into force in 1948 and replaced the 1897 Workmen's Compensation Act. It provides benefits at the rate of £8.75 a week for an adult plus £3.70 for an adult dependant, and children's allowances continuing for a maximum of 26 weeks. Permanent disablement benefit is assessed according to the degree of incapacitation.

There are a number of supplementary benefits, ranging upwards from £4, including allowances for special hardship, constant attendance, exceptionally severe disablement, hospital treatment and unemployability. Survivors' benefits are the same as in the general scheme.

Retirement and other pensions

There are two retirement pensions schemes — basic and graduated. Pensions are payable at normal age 65 for men and 60 for women. In the basic scheme the standard flat rate is £6 a week for a single person and £9.70 for a married couple, increased on late retirement by 6p per week for every 9 full rate contributions paid after retiring age. There are allowances for children. Under the graduated pension scheme, for which all Class 1 people earning over £9 per week are eligible, contributions are 4.75 per cent of weekly earnings between £18 and £42. Employers and employees pay the same contributions. The amount is 5p per week for every £30 contribution (men) and £36 (women). Employers may 'contract out' of the scheme in respect of earnings between £9 and £18 a week, provided that they operate a pensions scheme which guarantees an equivalent income. Many employers make private pensions provisions, which usually allow for pensions up to one-half to two-thirds of final salary for long service. Full tax relief can be obtained for contributions.

A death grant of £30 (standard) is payable.

Widows, after 26 weeks, receive £6 weekly plus allowances for dependent children — £2.95 per week for the eldest, £2.05 for the second and £1.95 for other children. During the first 26 weeks of bereavement, she will receive an allowance of £8.40 a week.

Family and maternity allowances

The maternity allowance is £6 per week plus dependants' allowances, beginning 11 weeks before confinement and ending six weeks after. There is a £25.00 maternity grant for each child born.

Family allowances are paid for the second child and subsequent children, normally up to age 15. Monthly benefits range from £3.90 for the second, and £4.33 for the third and subsequent children. The scheme is financed out of taxation.

A new benefit, introduced in August 1971, provides a family income supplement to help low-paid families and single people. This weekly supplement is appropriate for families with one child earning in total £18 or less. This earnings limit is raised by £2 per week for each additional child. The total weekly supplement may not exceed £4.

Unemployment benefit

Unemployment benefit is paid at a flat rate of £6.75 per week, after three days, for a period of 312 days. There are additional allowances for wives and dependant adults and children. There is also an earnings-related scheme, paid after 12 waiting days, which lasts for 156 days and provides a benefit of one third of average weekly earnings between £9 and £30, up to a maximum of 85 per cent of average earnings.

Under the Ministry of Social Security Act 1966 supplementary benefits, replacing the previous national assistance system, are available to people whose income falls below a certain level, as defined in the act.

This section would not be complete without reference to the far-ranging responsibilities of local authorities in the fields of housing, public health, child welfare etc, and to the volume of social service activities carried out by innumerable voluntary bodies which complement the State and local authority actions. These organisations have been particularly active in caring for the old, the sick and children.

The UK has reciprocal social security arrangements with a number of countries – including, of the Ten, Denmark, Belgium, West Germany, Norway, France, Ireland and Italy.

LABOUR RELATIONS AND PROCEDURES

Recruitment and contracts of employment

The Department of Employment (formerly Ministry of Labour) is broadly responsible for all manpower and employment matters, including placing, manpower planning, youth vocational training, factory inspection, redundancy, Wages Councils, conciliation and arbitration, unemployment, disabled workers and advice on labour relations. It has a staff of about 30,000 and operates through nine regions, with a network of area offices.

The Department has 869 employment exchanges and maintains a professional and executive register for people with professional business and technical qualifications.

In an effort to eradicate the 'image' of the 1930s with their dole queues, to improve efficiency and make the service more human, the Department re-shaped the employment exchange system in 1971. As part of this process, it was decided to allow arrangements for unemployment benefit to be paid by post. It is not obligatory for an employer to engage employees through the agencies, which are free, and the number of fee-charging exchanges, particularly for office workers, has increased. An employer must notify the Department about redundancies. The exchanges can assist workers who take jobs away from home with resettlement and other allowances, including a free fare and a settling grant. Improved concessions have been introduced in an Employment Transfer scheme, designed to increase labour mobility, as well as helping redundant workers.

The Contracts of Employment Act, 1963, laying down statutory minimum periods of notice for workers and employers, was revised in the Industrial Relations Act 1971. An employer must give his employees written information about the terms of employment (pay, methods of payment, hours, holidays, sickness, pensions and length of notice). He must also assure the worker of his statutory right to join, or not to join, a union and explain grievance procedures. The length of notice has been extended beyond that provided in the 1963 act, to provide for one week after 13 weeks' employment, two after two years, four after five years, six after 10 years and eight after 15 years. Employees who work less than 21 hours a week, registered dock workers, merchant seamen, Crown servants and employees abroad are not covered.

Under the Redundancy Payments Act 1964, employees with a minimum length of service of two years are entitled to a lump sum payment (varying according to length of service) if they lose their jobs through technological causes and their employer cannot offer alternative work. The Redundancy Payments Act Fund is financed from employers' contributions.

Collective bargaining

Voluntary collective bargaining is the cornerstone of British industrial relations and the standard method of determining wages and conditions of work. There is no statutory national minimum wage, but in some low-paid and badly organised industries, there are Wages Councils, which lay down statutory minima. These Councils, the successors to the 1909 Trade Boards, operate in 50 different areas and cover about 3½ million workers in such industries as food, distribution, clothing and catering. Their recommendations, subject to the approval of the Secretary of State, are legally enforceable. Wages Councils are gradually being superseded in favour of normal voluntary methods.

Bargaining systems vary widely in different industries, but they usually follow agreed procedural rules and their settlements are taken as the standard for the whole industry. Industry-wide bargaining deals with minimum rates, working hours and holidays, and questions of work practices and adjustments are usually handled at factory level. There is thus a two-tier system, with national minima fixed at the top, and other payments negotiated at shop level. Piecework or payment by results systems are still dominant in engineering, textiles and other industries where individual output can be measured. But in the more modern and capital-intensive industries, where the pace of production is set by the machine, the trend has been towards job evaluation and the adoption of standard rates for different grades. Some large firms have their own separate negotiating machinery and do not take part in national negotiations.

In the period 1958 to 1967, an average of about 3¼ million working days were lost annually through disputes. Since then the number of stoppages has risen sharply as indicated in Table 12.9.

During the first five months of 1972, there were 935 disputes involving 723,400 workers and causing a loss of 14,400,000 working days. The figure included the long-drawn out strike of coal miners in February. The largest number of working days lost since 1958 have been in the engineering and transport groups.

	No of disputes	No of workers 000s	Days lost 000s
1958	2,629	523	3,462
1968	2,378	2,255	4,690
1969	3,116	1,654	6,846
1970	3,906	1,793	10,980
1971	2,228	1,171	13,551

Source: Department of Employment Gazette

TABLE 12.9 Industrial Disputes and Days Lost

Apart from major official strikes, where most workers get strike pay, there has been a steady increase in the number of unofficial 'wild-cat' strikes, particularly in the car industry and in the docks. Unions also frequently make use of other types of industrial action, such as working to rule, and a phenomenon of 1971-72 has been the growth of workers 'sit-ins', usually in protest against unemployment or a threatened closure. Disputes over wages and conditions are the most frequent cause of strikes.

The pace-setter in new type negotiations was the agreement at Esso's

Fawley refinery with the Transport and General Workers Union reached in 1960. This embodies a 'productivity package deal' whereby, in return for increases of about 40 per cent in pay, the unions agreed to certain changes in working practices and to the more efficient utilisation of labour. This agreement was the forerunner of many productivity agreements reached during the 1960s.

Some collective contracts have written-in clauses about disputes procedures, but this is not universal. Industrial conciliation and mediation services are provided by the Department of Employment, whose officials may act when local attempts at a settlement have failed. They can step in when a conflict is developing or, if called upon by either party, can appoint a mediator. If conciliation fails, there is recourse to voluntary arbitration, which may take the form of reference to the industrial court, the appointment of individual arbiters or courts of enquiry. Compulsory arbitration was introduced during World War II, but ended in 1951. Many disputes are referred to special Committees or Courts of Inquiry. These bodies have no powers to enforce a settlement but their findings usually provide an acceptable basis for one.

Despite the elaborate peace-keeping machinery, the number of strikes has steadily risen, although the UK is by no means the most strike-hit country, as shown in Table 2.6.

Trade unions and employers

The main organisation for employers is the Confederation of British Industry, (CBI) formed as a result of the merger between the Federation of British Industries, the British Employers Confederation and the National Association of Manufacturers. There are about 1500 separate employers' associations, but most are federated to the CBI, which is the principal spokesman for industry in dealing with the TUC and the government. The CBI does not exercise bargaining functions, but gives general guidance and advice on all labour and industrial matters to its member firms. In July 1971, it secured a voluntary agreement that price increases during the coming twelve months would be limited to 5 per cent.

The British unions form the oldest and most powerful labour organisation in the free world, but owing to their historical and traditional background, they have developed on highly diverse and individualistic lines. Many are based on crafts and localities. In December 1971 there were 132 unions affiliated to the Trades Union Congress with a total membership of just under 10 million. The number of unions has slowly been diminishing, as a result of amalgamations, but the process of centralisation has not advanced, as in Germany and Scandinavia. There are occasional demarcation problems and competition between unions operating in the same field.

There are some very small unions and a few very large ones — Transport Workers (1.5 million members), Amalgamated Engineering and Foundry Workers (1.25 million members) and the General and Municipal Workers, with about 800,000. The commonest structural form is organisation by craft, or on a general basis, rather than the strictly industrial union, eg the Mineworkers. The most noteworthy feature of the last decade has been the declining strength of traditional sectors, eg mining, textiles and railways, and the growth of unions catering for white collar and professional workers.

The Trades Union Congress, like the CBI, co-ordinates the activities of its affiliated member unions and is a general policy-making body, but does not itself engage in collective bargaining and has little or no power over individual unions. While many manual workers' unions are affiliated to the Labour Party, the TUC, as such, has no party affiliations, and unions representing civil servants, local government officers and teachers do not participate in political activities. Executive powers reside in the General Council which is elected annually to represent various trade groups, and the administration comes under the TUC General Secretary and his staff at Congress House.

The basic unit of trade union organisation is the branch, based on locality, but the focal point is increasingly becoming the place of work. Here elected shop stewards have come to play a dominant role. As representatives of the workers, they take up grievances and act as spokesmen vis a vis management.

Because the job is arduous and time-consuming, there is a tendency for the more militant workers to stand for election. This has probably been one of the reasons for the growth of lightning strikes in the motor industry.

In the past, apart from the General Strike of 1926, industrial relations have been good in Britain, with the exception of a few industries. Since 1969, there has been an unsettled period, although most industries and firms remain free from strikes. In 1971 the government introduced the Industrial Relations Act. The purpose of this act is to bring some order into industrial relations by applying legal sanctions to certain forms of industrial action and providing better protection for the individual worker. The act has been bitterly opposed by the TUC largely on the grounds that it introduces legal elements into industrial relations. Affiliated unions were instructed by the TUC not to register under the act and to boycott such bodies as the Commission for Industrial Relations. 'The TUC's policy of non-cooperation is directed towards the act and not towards employers, with whom unions have to work jointly on a day-to-day basis' wrote Mr Victor Feather, TUC General Secretary, in a foreword to the TUC handbook on the act.

185

Nevertheless, relations between leaders of the two sides of industry remained friendly and during the summer of 1972 joint talks resulted in the setting up of a separate system of conciliation independent of the government.

Both sides of industry are represented on a number of official bodies, including the National Economic Development Council and the series of Economic Development Committees set up for individual industries.

Works councils

There is no formal system of workers' participation in industry. During the War, joint production committees played an important role, but the strength and status of the postwar consultative committees has declined. The British unions are against any statutory provision for consultation, on the German lines, and are more concerned about the pay packet than theories about industrial democracy. There is, however, a growing recognition among managements of the need to keep their workpeople informed about company developments, whether through formal or informal arrangements. Some firms operate profit-sharing schemes, as a means of enlisting the workers' support and interest, but the acquisition of shares has not developed to the same extent as in some EEC countries.

Within a factory, the personnel manager exerts a key role in maintaining good relationships. Many managements are now giving increased status and authority to these officers.

Employers have a duty at common law to provide a safe system of working and to observe the standards laid down for safety and health by Parliament. Statutory provisions for the health and safety of workers in factories are contained in the Factories Act 1961 and its supporting orders and regulations which are administered by the Department of Employment's Factory Inspectorate. There is also legislation relating to conditons in offices, shops and railway premises.

The urgent need for more attention to be focussed on safety was highlighted by the Robens report, July 1972, which pointed out that every year about 1,000 people are killed and half a million injured at their place of work. As for occupational health, about 650 factories have full time doctors and 4,300 have part time doctors. Research into industrial health problems and hazards is undertaken by a number of occupational health centres, the Medical Research Council, and other organisations.

Appendix 1

Sources of Information and Bibliography

The following publications have been invaluable as sources of information in the preparation of this book, and are recommended to all who wish to pursue the subject of employment conditions in Europe, in greater depth. A number of additional publications are also listed.

1 European Economic Community

The EEC Information Office (23 Chesham Street, London SW1) contains most of the main documents in its Library, where material can be consulted. Sales of official Community publications are handled by HMSO.

Official publications include EEC 'Journal officiel' (not yet available in English), general reports on the activities of the Community (annual), occasional studies on various aspects of the EEC and a series of statistics, which are obtainable on subscription.

Following are some of the general publications:

The Common Market and the Common Man, 4th edition, June 1972
Basic Statistics (1970)
European Community – monthly journal of EEC

A social policy programme in the Community, 1971

The enlarged Community in figures, 1972

Comparative table of the social security systems of EEC countries, 1970

European Community, The Facts, 1971

Annual reports of the Commission, the European Investment Bank, and reports on selected aspects of employment, regional policy, social affairs etc

2   General Reading:

'Community Europe Today', Broad and Jarrett, Wolff 1972 (£1.50)

Daily Telegraph, Guide to the Common Market, 1972 (50p)

Who does what in the Common Market, Mitchell and Burt, no 1 1972 (75p)

A readers' guide to Britain and the European Communities, C.A. Cosgrove, Chatham House/PEP, 1970 (75p)

The economics of the Common Market, D. Swann, Penguin (40p)

Barclays Bank Ltd, Britain and The Common Market, 1972

Lloyds Bank Ltd, What About Europe Now? 1972

Midland Bank Ltd, Facts About the Common Market, 1971

National Westminster Bank Ltd, Common Market and the UK (1970)

Sixteen Europeans look ahead, Fontana/Collins, by Richard Mayne, Chatham House/PEP 1972

The Times, Common Market, discussion pamphlets, Times, 1971

Fact sheets on Britain and Europe, obtainable from the Post Office

Europe and You, set of leaflets obtainable from Conservative Central Office, also CPC Notes on current politics.

Union Bank of Switzerland: Prices and Earnings around the globe, Zurich 1971

3   UK Official Publications

The United Kingdom and the European Communities (White Paper), July 1971, 25p

Britain and Europe, a short version of the White Paper, from Post Office, free

The Treaty of Rome, HMSO 1967, £1.20

Department of Trade and Industry:
    Britain and the EEC, 1971
    DTI Journal
    Hints to businessmen (discontinued)
Department of Employment:
    Department of Employment Gazette, monthly
    Various reports on Industrial Relations in Britain, and statistical material
        issued periodically
Central Office of Information (see also under UK)
    Series of reference documents

4   Confederation of British Industry

Signposts to the EEC, April 1972 (£3)
Britain in Europe, Jan. 1970 (£1.50)
European living costs compared, 1972 (£5)
CBI briefs:
    Small firms and the Common Market, 1971 (50p)
    Industrial standards in Europe, 1971 (50p)
    EEC Common Transport policy, 1971 (50p)
    Company Law Harmonisation Measures, 1971 (50p)
    Working in Europe, industrial relations 1972 (50p)
    Regional policy and the EEC, 1972 (50p)
    Vocational training and the European Social Fund 1972 (50p)

Other publications obtainable from the CBI, 21 Tothill Street, London SW1H 9LP.

5   Investment

Business Monitor, M 4 Overseas Transactions, HMSO
Government and Business, article by Professor J.H. Dunning, December 1971
Banking developments in Europe, P. Readman, Gower Press 1973

6   Social Security

A guide to social security in Europe, Noble Lowndes International Ltd, 1972
Social Insurance News, Assicurazioni Generali, Trieste, 1972

7 Labour Relations and Procedures

Labour relations and employment conditions, Coventry and District Employers Association, 1972 (£2.50)

C.E.D. Samson, Brussels, Obligations sociales employeurs, 1972

Trade unions and the free movement of Labour, R. Colin Beever, Chatham House/PEP 1969 (37½p)

Unions in Europe, Kendall and Marx, Centre for Contemporary European Studies, Sussex University, 1971 (30p)

Institute of Personnel Management:
  Implications of European integration for Personnel Management, IPM Information report no 6, 1970

The EEC and UK Engineering Companies, British Mechanical Engineering Confederation in association with 'Engineering' Industrial Press Ltd, 1971 (£15.75)

The EEC and the migration of workers, W.R. Bohning and David Stephen, Runnymede Trust, 1971 (25p)

The migration of workers in the UK and the European Community, W.R. Bohning, Institute of Race Relations and Oxford University Press, 1972 (£3.00)

New Community, October 1971. Community Relations commission

International Labour Office: Bulletin of Labour Statistics, 1972, Geneva (8 Swiss francs)

International Labour Review: articles on Collective bargaining in various European countries, 1971 (£0.30 per issue):
  Recent trends in collective bargaining in:

Netherlands, W.Albeda	March 1971
France, Y.Delamotte	April 1971
Belgium, R.Blanpain	July—August 1971
Italy, G.Giugni	October 1971
Federal Republic of Germany, H. Reichel	December 1971

8 Management

Top Management Remuneration, Europe 1970, Management Centre Europe

Comparative tax tables, Europe, Management Counsellors International

Company sponsored benefit programmes in the EEC, Management Counsellors International

9   Individual Countries

In general, the information contained in the surveys of the Ten countries is derived from material supplied by Embassies, Government departments, official reviews and surveys, press and periodical articles, background notes, reports and pamphlets provided by different organisations and individuals. It is not possible to list these in detail, but mention must be made of:

Business briefing for Belgium, British Chamber of Commerce, Brussels
Labor law and practice in Belgium, US Labor department, Sept. 1969
OECD, Economic surveys
Italy — Traits essentiels de la protection du travail, Confederazione generale dell'industria, 1972
Netherlands — Work and prosperity, Pathus and Van der Spek, 1970
    Facts and figures series issued by Ministry of Foreign Affairs
UK 'Britain 1972', Central Office of Information, HMSO 1971 (£1.80)
    Reference pamphlets of the COI and other material
    The employment of British workers in Germany D.E.
Denmark — Industrial Participation, Spring 1972, article by E. Ohrt on Joint consultation in Danish industry. (Industrial Co-partnership Association)

10   Other Sources

Europa Yearbook, 1972, Europa Publications Ltd
Parliamentary debates, Hansard
The Times
The Daily Telegraph
The Financial Times
The Guardian
The Economist
The Investors' Chronicle

and other newspapers and periodicals carry frequent surveys and articles on various aspects of the EEC.

Appendix 2

Useful Addresses in London and Europe

1   EEC

European Economic Community – The Commission (all main divisions)
1040 Brussels, 200 rue de la Loi
010.32.2.35.00.40/35.80.40

EEC Statistical Office
Centre Louvigny, Luxembourg
010.352.288.31

EEC Economic and Social Committee, as for The Commission

European Coal and Steel Community
3 Boulevard Joseph II
Luxembourg
010.352.288.31

European Investment Bank
2 Place de Metz
Luxembourg
043.50.11
Representative office in Brussels:
Rue Royale 60, 1000 Brussels
13.40.00

Delegation of the Commission of the EEC to the UK
20 Kensington Palace Gardens, London W 8
01.229.9633/7/8

Information Office of the EEC
23 Chesham Street, London SW1X 8NH
01.235.4904

The UK Permanent Representative at the EEC
51/52 Avenue des Arts, Brussels 1040
01.32.2.13.77.80

The Commission has delegations in Geneva, Paris, Washington, New York, Santiago and Montevideo. For addresses, see 'Who does what in the Common Market' Mitchell and Birt, no 1.

2   United Kingdom Government

Department of Trade and Industry

1 Victoria Street, SW1H OET
01.222.7877
EEC enquiries ext. 3579 and 2479
EFTA enquiries ext. 2480 and 2479

Export Services Division
50 Ludgate Hill, EC4M 7HU
01.248.5757
Intelligence: 01.248.9633

Regional Industrial Development Division
Room 737, Millbank Tower
SW1P 4QU
01.834.2255 ext. 418

Department of Employment

8 St James's Square
SW1Y 4JR
01.930.6200

Overseas division
32 St James's Square
SW1Y 4JR
01.930.6200

Department of Health and Social Security

> Alexander Fleming House
> Elephant and Castle
> SE1
> 01.407.5522

Foreign and Commonwealth Office

> European Integration Department
> Downing Street
> SW1
> 01.930.2323

Central Office of Information

> Hercules Road
> Westminster Bridge Road
> SE1
> 01.928.2345

HM Stationery Office

> Government Bookshop
> 49 High Holborn
> WC1V 6HB
> Other bookshops in Edinburgh, Cardiff, Manchester, Bristol, Birmingham
> and Belfast

3   London Organisations

Employment Conditions Abroad Ltd
9 Orme Court
London W2 4RL
01.229.3262

Confederation of British Industry
21 Tothill Street
SW1H 9LP
01.930.6711

Regional secretaries in Leeds, South-east, Birmingham, Newcastle-upon
Tyne, Belfast, Manchester, Glasgow, Bristol and Cardiff.
Addresses from CBI, or see Signposts to Europe, p 48

Trades Union Congress
Congress House
Great Russell Street
WC1 B 3LS
01.636.4030

British Institute of Management
Management House
Parker Street
WC2B 5PT
01.405.3456

Institute of Personnel Management
5 Winsley Street
Oxford Circus
W1N 7AQ
01.580.3271

Industrial Co-partnership Association
60 Buckingham Gate
SW1
01.828.8754/5

Institute of Directors
10 Belgrave Square
SW1
01.235.3601

Industrial Society
Robert Hyde House
43 Bryanston Square
W1H 8AH
01.262.2401

4 British Embassies in the Enlarged Community

BELGIUM:
Britannia House, Rue Joseph II, 28 B-1040, BRUSSELS
(191165, 181709, 187600)
Consulate in Antwerp

FRANCE:
    35 rue du Faubourg St Honore, Paris 8e
    (265.2710/5, 265.06 20/4)
    Consulates in Bordeaux, Lille, Lyon, Marseille and Strasbourg

GERMANY:
    53 BONN Friedrich-Ebert Allee 77
    (234061)
    Consulates in Berlin, Dusseldorf, Frankfurt, Hamburg, Hanover, Munich,
    Stuttgart

ITALY:
    Via XX Settembre 80A, I-00187 ROME
    (4755551-5)
    Consulate-General MILAN, Via San Paolo 7, I-20121
    Consulates in Florence, Genoa, Naples, Palermo, Turin, Venice

LUXEMBOURG:
    28 Boulevard Royal, Luxembourg
    (29864/5)

NETHERLANDS:
    Lange Voorhout 10, THE HAGUE
    (070 64.58.00)
    Consulate-General, Amsterdam
    Johannes Vermeerstraat, 0.2
    (020 73.91.43)

DENMARK:
    38-40 Kastelsvej, DK-2100 COPENHAGEN Ø
    (Tria 6360)

IRISH REPUBLIC:
    30 Merrion Square, DUBLIN 2
    (65678/9)

NORWAY:
    Thomas Heftyesgate 8 OSLO 2,
    (56.38.90/7)
    Consulate in Bergen

For addresses of Consulates, contact the Embassy Commercial Department, or see CBI Signposts to the EEC pp 51/2.
    Labour attaches are based in Bonn, Paris, Belgium (covering Netherlands,

Luxembourg and EEC) and Sweden, (covering Denmark and Norway.

5   London Embassies of The Ten

BELGIUM:
Belgian Embassy
103 Eaton Square
SW1 W 9AB
01-235 5422

FRANCE:
French Embassy
58 Knightsbridge
SW1
01-235 8080

GERMANY:
Embassy of the Federal Republic of Germany
23 Belgrave Square
SW1X 8PZ
01-235 5033

Commercial Information
6 Rutland Gate
SW7 1AY
01-584 1271

ITALY:
Italian Embassy
14 Three King's Yard
W1
01-629 8200

Commercial Office
31 Old Burlington St.
W1
01-734 2411

LUXEMBOURG:
Luxembourg Embassy
27 Wilton Crescent
SW1X 8SD
01-235 6961

NETHERLANDS:
   Royal Netherlands Embassy
   38 Hyde Park Gate
   SW7 5DP
   01-584 5040

DENMARK:
   Royal Danish Embassy
   67 Pont Street
   SW1X OBQ
   01-584 0102

IRELAND:
   Irish Embassy
   17 Grosvenor Place
   SW1X 7HR
   01-235 2171

NORWAY:
   Royal Norwegian Embassy
   25 Belgrave Square
   SW1X 8QD
   01-235 7151

Labour Attaches are attached to Embassies of France, Germany and Italy.

6   European Chambers of Commerce in UK

BELGIUM:
   Belgian Chamber of Commerce in Great Britain (Inc)
   6 Belgrave Square
   SW 1X 8PM
   01-235 3255

FRANCE:
   French Chamber of Commerce in Great Britain
   Park House
   24 Rutland Gate
   SW7 1BB
   01- 584 9628

GERMANY:
German Chambers of Industry and Commerce
11 Grosvenor Crescent
SW1X 7EE
01-235 9947

Federation of German Industries
33 Bruton Street
W1X 8DR
01-499 5852

ITALY:
Italian Chamber of Commerce for Great Britain
31 Old Burlington Street
W1X 2DQ
01-734 2411

NETHERLANDS:
Chamber of Commerce in UK
307/8 High Holborn
WC1V 7LS
01-405 1358

NORWAY:
Norwegian Chamber of Commerce
21-24 Cockspur Street
SW1Y 5BN
01-930 0181

7   British Chambers of Commerce & Similar Bodies

The British Chamber of Commerce for Belgium and Luxembourg
30 Rue Joseph II,
Brussels, 4 BELGIUM
190788

British Import Union
Borsbygningen
1217 Copenhagen K
DENMARK

The British Chamber of Commerce, France Inc
6 rue Halevy
Paris IX
FRANCE
073 4921

British Trade Council in Germany
c/o Commercial Department
British Embassy, Bonn
GERMANY

The British Chamber of Commerce for Italy
Via Tarchetti 1/3 20121
Milan, ITALY
20121

Netherlands British Chamber of Commerce
PO Box 2804
45 Raamweg
The Hague NETHERLANDS
070-184668

8   Other European Organisations

International Labour Office
CH 1211 Geneva 22
SWITZERLAND
31.24.00 - 32.62.00

London office: 40 Piccadilly, W1
            01-734 6521

Regional offices in France, Germany and Italy

OECD, Organisation for Economic Cooperation and Development
Publications, 2 rue Andre-Pascal, Paris 7e

Obtainable from HMSO

International Confederation of Free Trade Unions (ICFTU)
and European Confederation of Free Trade Unions (ECFTUC)
Brussels 1000, 34/51 rue Montagne aux herbes potageres
010.32.2.17.9141

Management Counsellors International SA
Avenue Louise 209a 1050 Brussels, Belgium
49.95.05

Management Centre Europe
Avenue des Arts 4
Brussels 1040, Belgium
19.03.90

International Organisation of Employers
98 rue de St Jean
Geneva Switzerland
31.73.50

Annex

Redundancy Procedures

Many dismissals of labour are the result of structural changes in industry and of the introduction of automative processes. Redundancies may be on an individual or a collective basis, and in every EEC country there is provision to cushion the effects. The systems vary widely, and the Commission in the summer of 1972 submitted to the Council of Ministers proposals for establishing common rules for dismissal and guidelines for future policies, which would protect the workers without impeding industrial change.

1   Individual dismissal

Legal provisions exist in most countries (Germany, Italy, Luxembourg and the Netherlands) to safeguard a worker against unjustified dismissal, although in all the Six, dismissal without notice is accepted in the event of a serious offence.

In Belgium and Italy, notice must be given in writing, in France and Luxembourg, by registered letter and verbally in Germany and the Netherlands.

Length of notice varies according to age and length of service. For the minority of manual workers, it is one week to one month, and for the majority, one to six months. For the minority of white collar workers, it is one to three months, and for the majority six months to two years. In all countries, except the Netherlands, white collar workers are entitled to longer notice than manual workers.

All countries stipulate that workers' representatives should be informed and consulted about dismissals. In Germany the works council must by law be consulted.

In Italy and Luxembourg, the appropriate labour authorities have to be informed; in France and the Netherlands, they must give their authorisation, but in Belgium and Germany, the public authorities play practically no part.

France, Italy and Luxembourg grant legal minimum compensation, varying according to length of service. In Belgium, the Netherlands and Germany (except in the case of judicial termination of employment) there is no legal provision and compensation is normally arranged by negotiated agreement.

Provisions for re-employment in the same firm vary. In France, Germany and the Netherlands, this is possible, but not obligatory. In Belgium, it is provided only as a protection for workers' representatives. In Italy, payment of compensation and reinstatement are compulsory and wages must be paid during the intervening period. In Luxembourg, priority of re-employment must be given to dismissed workers.

In all Six countries, except the Netherlands, workers' representative bodies are entitled to legal and/or negotiated protection. In France, union delegates can only be dismissed with the approval of the Factory inspectorate.

All countries provide for temporary suspension of the contract in the case of sickness, accident, pregnancy and childbirth and have some arrangements for workers called up for military service.

2   Collective redundancy

In Germany, Belgium and Italy, this is defined on the basis of numbers employed and applies only to firms employing a given number of men (21 in Germany, 20-25 in Belgium and 11 in Italy). Mass redundancy occurs when a given number of dismissals are made – 6-50 in Germany, 25 per cent in Belgium, 10 in Luxembourg. The Netherlands do not specify an exact number but refer to 'a relatively high number within a short period'. The French have a rather wider definition, applying the term to all dismissals 'for economic or technical reasons', eg lack of raw materials, a change in the state of the market, reorganisation, new methods or the closing down of some departments. A distinction is made between dismissals arising from economic conditions and those due to amalgamation, concentration or restructuring. The Italian system is based on an interconfederal agreement, and makes provision for conciliation in firms with 6-10 workers and the intervention of workers' representatives in firms employing over 10 workers.

Procedures vary, but are usually laid down in negotiated agreements. In all cases, provision (by law or agreement) is made for the works council to be notified and for consultation on methods for avoiding the redundancies.

In three countries (Germany, Belgium and Luxembourg) the appropriate labour authorities must be informed, and in France and the Netherlands their authorisation is obligatory. In Italy the Department of Labour usually seeks to use conciliation.

Compensation for mass redundancies varies from country to country; most arrangements are made by collective bargaining. Belgium makes special payments if a firm with more than 25 workers is closed. In Italy, employers are legally obliged to pay redundant workers for 180 days an amount equal to two-thirds of their former wages.

In Italy and Luxembourg there is a law providing priority reinstatement for dismissed workers, if there is a revival of employment. In Belgium and France, priority for dismissed workers is provided for in negotiated agreements. In Germany and the Netherlands, this is possible but not obligatory.

3   The United Kingdom

Procedures for compensation are laid down in the Redundancy Payments Act 1965. This is paid at the basic rate of one week's pay for each complete year of service, but no payment is made for less than 2 years' service, service under 18 or over 65. The maximum period to count for compensation is 20 years service. Service between 18 and 21 attracts half a week's pay per year of service, and over 40, one and a half week's pay. The maximum wage or salary is £40 a week.

A Redundancy Fund has been established, to which all employers contribute a fixed amount per week per employee. They can claim a rebate from the fund, after a redundancy has been effected, varying according to age.

The Department of Employment must be given not less than 14 days' notice of the termination date of a redundant employee.

Higher rates of compensation may often be negotiated. Compensation may also take the form of increased pensions, especially for older workers.

Disputes may be referred to an Industrial Tribunal.

There is no definition of mass redundancy, but when redundancy for ten or more workers within one week is planned, the Department must be given at least 21 days' notice.

All employees have protection against unfair dismissal, and dismissal must be for a good reason. The legal minimum length of notice is one week rising to six weeks after ten years and eight weeks after 15 years service. Staff workers customarily have contracts entitling them to one month's notice, increased to three to six months according to seniority.

4   The Commission's Proposals

The proposals, under review by the Council of Ministers, are part of the 'harmonisation' process. They include:

. . the obligation of a firm to inform the worker in writing of the reasons for his dismissal,
. . a period of at least six week's notice before dismissal, with three months for workers over 40 and six months for those over 50,
. . compensation, beyond the salary due, to be paid out of special funds coordinated at Community level,
. . consultation with workers' representatives about ways of avoiding redundancies, rather than merely explaining the reasons,
. . special protection for workers' representatives, elderly or disabled workers,
. . an agreed definition of mass or 'collective' redundancy, eg the dismissal of more than ten per cent of the workers in a firm employing 50-500 workers over four weeks, and of the circumstances in which this would be allowed, eg the closing of a factory. Employers would not be allowed to take on new workers during this period.

The Commission stresses the need for coordinated action to provide 'continuity of employment' and for measures of re-training, so that a dismissed worker can find a new job as soon as possible.